TWENTIETH CENTURY LIBRARY

Twentieth Century Library

Fyodor Dostoevsky

TWENTIETH CENTURY LIBRARY
HIRAM HAYDN, EDITOR

Published:

JAMES JOYCE by W. Y. Tindall
CHARLES DARWIN by Paul B. Sears
ALBERT EINSTEIN by Leopold Infeld
GEORGE BERNARD SHAW by Edmund Fuller
FYODOR DOSTOEVSKY by Rene Fueloep-Miller
WILLIAM JAMES by Lloyd Morris

★

In Preparation:

KARL MARX by Max Lerner
SIGMUND FREUD by Gregory Zilboorg
JOHN DEWEY by Jerome Nathanson
FRANZ BOAS by Melville J. Herskovits
OSWALD SPENGLER by H. Stuart Hughes
ALFRED NORTH WHITEHEAD by Stanley Newburger
MOHANDAS K. GANDHI by Haridas T. Muzumdar

CHARLES SCRIBNER'S SONS

RENÉ FUELOEP-MILLER

Fyodor Dostoevsky

INSIGHT, FAITH, AND PROPHECY

TRANSLATED BY

RICHARD AND CLARA WINSTON

CHARLES SCRIBNER'S SONS, NEW YORK

CHARLES SCRIBNER'S SONS, LTD., LONDON

1950

CONTENTS

PART I
DOSTOEVSKY—THE MAN AND HIS WORK

PART II
DOSTOEVSKY'S SIGNIFICANCE FOR OUR TIMES

PART I

DOSTOEVSKY—THE MAN AND HIS WORK

CHAPTER ONE

DOSTOEVSKY'S UNFINISHED WORK

A PROLOGUE

PETERSBURG—the night of April 11, 1880, by the Russian calendar. Outside the sky was growing lighter, and still Dostoevsky sat at his desk—a man of sixty with a sallow face lined by illness and sorrow, framed in a long, tangled beard. Beside him stood the cold samovar and a tray filled with ashes and cigarette stubs.

He had worked through the night to complete the tenth section of *The Brothers Karamazov*—"The Boys"—for the next issue of the *Russian Messenger*. For weeks, for months, he had bent over his novel night after night. This was the first moment he had a chance to relax.

A pile of neglected correspondence lay on his desk. At the bottom was a letter he had long particularly wanted to answer. It was from a young woman, a painter, who suffered from her inner duality and was appealing to him, the great psychologist, for help. Dostoevsky, who was also at variance with himself, recognized in the woman a kindred spirit. In his reply to Mademoiselle N. N. he opened his heart without restraint. His letter was a confession that revealed this martyred writer's tragic secret of creation.

"My life passes in such disorder and haste that I belong to myself only on the rarest occasions," he wrote. "Even now, when I at last have a moment to write to you, I shall be able to say

3

only a fraction of all that weighs upon me. . . . I know that as a writer I have many faults, nor am I ever satisfied with myself. I must confess to you that in the anguished moments when I try to draw up a reckoning with myself, I reach the painful conclusion that in all my works I have not said the twentieth part of what I have to say and perhaps could say. . . . I feel there is so much more in me than what I have hitherto managed to express in my writing."

When Dostoevsky wrote this letter, he had already completed more than twenty novels and tales. His major works, *Notes from Underground, Crime and Punishment, The Idiot, The Possessed, A Raw Youth,* among others, were already written, and his last work and masterpiece, *The Brothers Karamazov,* was nearing completion. One of the most significant achievements in modern literature was virtually finished; the world Dostoevsky had created, the world of Raskolnikov, Myshkin, Stavrogin, and now of the Karamazovs and the Grand Inquisitor, had come into being like a cosmos complete in itself.

But he had not yet mined the greater treasure. And at that moment of personal audit all his unwritten works troubled his artist's conscience.

A decade and a half had passed since Dostoevsky wrote *Crime and Punishment.* It was the first novel in the group of works in which he attempted to frame his fundamental philosophical idea: the falling away from God in crime and the way to salvation through purification. Raskolnikov's will to power does not stop even at murder, and leads to disaster; his crime brings down his punishment; only repentance shows him the way to rebirth.

On the threshold of the new life, the novel breaks off. "But that is the beginning of a new story," the book ends, "the story of the gradual renewal of a man, the story of his regeneration . . . of his initiation into a new, unknown life."

This new story was to form a second volume. It is but one of Dostoevsky's many unwritten works.

Some ten years earlier Dostoevsky had conceived the plan of an epic cycle of novels comprising many volumes, like Balzac's

Comédie humaine. His would be *The Life of a Great Sinner.* In it he intended to take up once more the theme he had left unfinished in *Crime and Punishment,* and portray the life of a man who veers between the two poles of the soul—defection from God in sin and harmony in God. He projected a dramatic theodicy in which he would synthesize all his poetic and ethical ideas and lay bare the hidden inner beauty, the ultimate divine source, behind all the chaos and confusion of living. All his previous books seemed to him mere prefaces to this great novel. It would be, he declared, the supreme goal of his life. "Once I have written this novel I shall gladly die," he cried in his first enthusiasm.

Nine pages in a notebook—a sketchy outline, a few traits of characters, the motifs of scenes, fragmentary dialogues—that is all we have of this "testament to humanity." Very likely some of the most important figures in his later novels derived from this project: Stavrogin, Kirillov, Arcady Dolgoruki, the pilgrim Makar Ivanovitch, Kolya Krashovsky, Ivan and Alyosha Karamazov. But at most these were precious slivers from the imposing structure of *The Life of a Great Sinner.* Dostoevsky himself felt only too painfully that his finished works were paltry compared to the original conception. For in his self-criticism he matched reality against his sweeping vision.

But that was not all that gnawed his conscience in the agony of self-examination. The drawer in which he kept his disordered notebooks was full of unfinished sketches and fragments. These included the outline of a novel about a philanthropic old-clothes dealer, the beginning of a short novel entitled *The Death of a Writer,* sketches for the story of a dishonored girl, and a detailed plan for a historical novel, *The Emperor,* whose hero was to be a Russian Kaspar Hauser. Many of the dearest ideas that sprang from his rich imagination lay interred in these notebooks.

Most painful of all was that small envelope on which he had noted, four years before on Christmas Eve, a "memento for my whole life"—the books he was determined still to write: "1) A Russian *Candide.* 2) My memoirs. 3) A book on Jesus Christ and 4) The Commemoration of the Dead. All this," he had written underneath, "and in addition the last novel [*The Brothers Kara-*

mazov], and the edition of *The Diary* I want to prepare, will require at least ten years of work and—I am now fifty-six."

Of those ten years, four had already passed. They had "gone by as in a dream." Of the books noted in this memorandum he had done no more than the sketchy beginning of his memoirs, a few issues of *The Diary of a Writer*, and only a part of his novel.

"What keeps me going is solely the hope that some day God will grant me so much inspiration and strength that I shall be able to say all that lies locked in my heart and my imagination." So ends this passage in Dostoevsky's letter to Mademoiselle N. N.

The Brothers Karamazov promised to fulfill this hope. Its tremendous framework gave its creator the chance to fuse his still fluid ideas into a great vision. By resolving the "Karamazov indignation" in terms of divine harmony, he could put in its conclusive form this thought which had occupied him all his life. True, his health was poor; he suffered from epileptic fits; his pulmonary emphysema, an old trouble, was getting worse; he was weighed down by a multitude of material cares and obligations; but all these difficulties could not quench his creative fire. He was devoting all his energies to the completion of this last "crowning work." For months he sat at his desk "without raising his head." "I have neglected everything, even my most sacred duties, not to speak of myself, solely in order to bring my work to completion," he wrote in a letter of October 15, 1880. "It is six o'clock in the morning; the city is awakening, but I have not yet gone to bed, and the doctors tell me I must not wear myself out with work and sit stooped over my desk for ten or twelve hours without a break."

On November 8 he was at last able to send the final section of his novel to the *Russian Messenger*. *The Brothers Karamazov* in the form we know it was finished. But the subject he had planned to treat was far from exhausted. In the sensualist, Fyodor Pavlovitch, Dostoevsky had shown the corruption of the old way of life; in the sons—the heirs of that depravity—he portrayed the dawning perception that faith alone could save them. The youngest of the brothers, the novice Alyosha, is closest to salvation. He is sent out into the world by his spiritual master, Elder Zossima; there his mission is to fulfill the idea of Christ amid the problems of daily life. Alyosha's address to the schoolboys at the close of the book is a symbolic indication of the importance of his mission for the future of mankind.

In the second volume Dostoevsky had planned to make Alyosha the principal figure; the book was to portray both the perfection of a man renewed by faith and the world-transforming power emanating from such a man. The theme of this book was to be the life of a Christ who is not crucified, but carries out his mission and modulates the discord of this world into divine harmony.

Dostoevsky set to work with fervor on this second volume. It would, he felt, round out his life. He had been at it barely three months when, on the night of January 16, 1881, the pen fell from his hand while he was writing. He bent to pick it up. The hasty movement caused a hemorrhage. Two days later he died.

Thus his last and most important work remained half-finished, half-unfinished, bearing out the gloomy premonition he had spoken of in one of his letters thirteen years before: "I shall die without having communicated the most important part of my ideas."

CHAPTER TWO

THE NOVEL OF HIS LIFE

HIS failure to complete this work was but the last tragic touch in Dostoevsky's creative career. Parallel with all the written and unwritten books, the worlds of fantasy that Dostoevsky created or planned, runs the great novel that filled his every day and night, every fiber of his nervous system, his whole ego—the novel of his life. All the problems that beset the heroes of his novels—the ultimate mystery of existence, the coming to grief of the guilty and innocent, blind chance and higher destiny—the problems take on a profounder, more dramatic significance when we see them in the light of this extraordinary life. For here, upon the plane of ordinary existence, the greatest of all dramas was being played: the divine drama of the crucifixion, of the passion of the spirit nailed to the cross of sluggish matter.

From the beginning to the end of his artistic career the curse of physical and psychic suffering hung over Dostoevsky. Although his works deal profoundly with serious questions, their wild and arbitrary occurrences, their often improbable tragic coincidences, their stark contrasts and melodramatic exaggerations, sometimes give them the tone of thrillers or detective stories. But these melodramatic elements were part and parcel of the tragedy of his own life, which reads almost as if Dostoevsky had invented it himself.

Dostoevsky completed his first novel, *Poor Folk*, in a wretched flat in Petersburg. During the writing he had often lived on barley and water, or, when he could get credit from the grocer, on milk and bread. He had only recently finished the book when, at four o'clock one morning, there came a violent knocking on his door. Into the room rushed his friend Grigorovitch and the poet Nekrassov. They had sat up all night reading Dostoevsky's manuscript to one another. "You don't know what you've written; you're a genius, a genius!" Nekrassov burst out. Soon afterward he announced, "A new Gogol has arisen among us," when he recommended Dostoevsky to the redoubtable Russian critic Belinsky.

Overnight Dostoevsky became a celebrated Russian author. He wrote nine more tales, among them *The Double, The Landlady*, and *A Feeble Soul*, and his mind was teeming with plans for many others. "I have a host of ideas for novels. I am writing without pause. My heart is atremble with all the new characters that spring into being in my mind. Never before have I had such clarity, such inner wealth," he wrote to his brother.

Two installments of one of these planned novels, *Netotchka Nezvanova*, had already been published. He was working on the third installment. Then, very late at night, there was again a knock at the door—this time to put a sudden end to his work. A gendarme, a lieutenant, and several Cossacks strode into his room with clanking sabers. "In the name of the law," the head of the detachment cried. The Cossacks rummaged through his papers and sealed them.

Accused of political conspiracy, Dostoevsky was arrested and taken to the Peter and Paul Fortress. There he spent eight months awaiting trial. But his genius surmounted the darkness and cold of the solitary cell, the torment of interrogations, and the illness that racked him. After the first few months of enforced inactivity, he was permitted the use of writing materials. He at once set to work and wrote a psychological story, *The Little Hero*. At the same time he had many other plans. "I am not wasting my time in prison," he wrote. "I have thought out three new tales and two novels. On one of them I am now writing."

Then, on December 22, 1849, he was startled out of his concentration by unusual noise in the corridor. His cell door was opened, and he, together with nine other "conspirators," was led to the place of execution. The men were bound to stakes, the white shirts of the condemned were put on them, they were given the crucifix to kiss, and the sword was snapped over their heads. "I stood in the second group and was sixth in line. I had no more than a minute to live," he later wrote. "Then a white cloth was waved, the troops sounded retreat, and we were informed that His Majesty the Czar was graciously sparing our lives; the sentence of death was being commuted to four years at hard labor and six more years of Siberian penal servitude."

With all his wealth of new ideas, to go to Siberia and be buried alive—he could not at first bear the thought. "How shall I ever be able to write again?" he asked before he was transported.

On Christmas night he was chained, and with ten pounds of metal dragging at his ankles, sent off to Siberia.

Dostoevsky was twenty-four when he wrote his first novel, *Poor Folk*, and sixty when he composed his last, *The Brothers Karamazov*. Of his thirty-six years of literary activity, ten were spent in Siberian exile. "Four whole horrible years" he was behind prison walls in The House of the Dead, the Katorga at Omsk. "Eternally in chains, eternally under guard, eternally behind bolts and bars, and never alone! . . . Fetters and the total suppression of my mind—that was my life in the fortress."

The hardest penalties and humiliations were imposed upon him in the Katorga. He was an ordinary convict, branded on both arms with the criminal's mark of shame. One side of his head was kept shaved in mockery. He pounded alabaster under the overseer's lash, turned the whetstone, or carried bricks for the construction of a barracks at temperatures of forty degrees below zero. "Most of all, however, I suffered from not being permitted to write in prison, while at the same time the work was seething inside me."

It was at this time that the question first thrust itself upon him: What is crime, and what is the fate of men who overstep the permissible limits? The problem of guilt, crime, and punishment —a subject that no artist before him had treated out of his own experience—confronted him. As if of its own accord this subject

took shape in his mind, became the plot of a novel, characters and
scenes. The idea for the first version of *Crime and Punishment*
came to him during those years of suffering in the Katorga.

"In my mind I have created a big novel which I consider my
ultimate work," he reported. But he was tormented by fear "that
my first love for this novel—that love without which it is impossible to write—may grow cold in the passing of the years before
the hour of realization comes at last."

After four years he was released from his convict chains. But
the hour of realization had not yet come. He had to serve the rest
of his sentence as a common soldier in the Siberian garrison
of Semipalatinsk. The monotonous drilling and the strenuous
marches by day, the wearing night watches in the Siberian steppe,
prevented him for some time from getting to work.

Later he was permitted to take a room of his own in an *isba*
(hut) near the barracks, and thus he had the privilege of at least
a few hours of solitude after his spells of duty. Trembling with
excitement at once more holding a pen after so long a time, he
struck out on the project that had matured in his mind in prison.
But before he was fully launched on the work, it had once more
to be broken off.

"A circumstance, a chance that was long in the coming and
arrived at last, has overwhelmed and consumed me," he wrote
after his meeting with Maria Dmitrievna, the wife of a Siberian
official named Issayev. Dostoevsky, thirty-two years old, just
emerged from four womanless years in prison, had kindled instantly and fallen in love with her. At first his unexpected happiness kept him from working; later, when Maria had to follow her
husband to another Siberian village, the agony of separation prevented him from continuing his book. "I am convinced I should
now spoil everything that I worked out so carefully over the
years," he wrote resignedly, and he postponed writing the novel
until after his return from Siberia.

Since he was unable to master the larger work, he turned to
its opposite pole; instead of writing about the grave and difficult
problem of murder, he produced two stories in a lighter vein:
Uncle's Dream and the comic novel, *The Friend of the Family*.

Then, to put his experience of the Katorga to some sort of use, and, as it were, to appease his artistic conscience, he began a sort of reportage on the theme of imprisonment and criminality. This book, too—*The House of the Dead*—was star-crossed by love.

Maria Dmitrievna's husband had died. Yet when Dostoevsky wanted to marry her she confessed that, weary of their long separation, she had taken up with another man. In spite of this they were married; but when the pair left Siberia at the end of Dostoevsky's term, the lover whom Maria brought along as an appendage to their marriage came too, his coach keeping a few versts behind theirs. "Recently I have been so tormented," Dostoevsky wrote, "that it was impossible for me to do any work at all."

He had hoped that once free he would be able to bring his great Katorga novel to completion; in point of fact freedom became for him another sort of martyrdom. There yawned before the now-forgotten writer the gates of another Katorga—the prison of the daily struggle for existence. He started his new life penniless, and had to fight anew every step of the way.

Responsibilities laid new fetters upon him. "I have taken upon myself the burden of a family, and it is dragging me down," he admitted. For besides himself and his wife, he had to provide support for her unemployed lover and his adolescent stepson.

The magazine *Vremya*, which his brother Michael had founded, was in danger of folding up. For his brother's sake, Dostoevsky took over the onus of the editorial work with its time-consuming details. He attended to these duties as though he were at forced labor, staying in the office until six o'clock in the morning, cutting his sleep down to a few hours a day, writing articles, reading proofs, negotiating with authors and with the censor, correcting manuscripts, and answering letters. In such matters he frittered away all his energies.

He had intended to make his literary debut after Siberia with the novel *The Insulted and Injured*. Now, however, he worked at it with the thought of providing exciting installments to attract new subscribers to the magazine. Even as he wrote he was painfully conscious of how far away this hastily scribbled "feuilleton," with its "puppets instead of people," was from the great novel he had envisioned in Siberia.

This exhausting struggle for a livelihood had for background Dostoevsky's doomed marriage. He paid a daily toll of new humiliations, furious quarrels, and equally stormy reconciliations. The scenes between husband and wife grew increasingly coarse because of Maria's heightened irritability—she was slowly dying of consumption—and his own more and more frequent attacks of epilepsy. It was a marital inferno, more terrible than the cruelest imagination could conceive: a half-insane invalid and an epileptic were torturing one another to death.

The strength the artist nevertheless managed to salvage from his wretchedness was just enough to enable him to complete his report on the Katorga—*The House of the Dead.*

Then he fell ill. His epilepsy, from which he had suffered since childhood, grew so much worse that the doctor urgently recommended a trip to western Europe for a rest.

"His situation is unimaginably desperate," the Governor General wrote at the time to the Minister of the Interior in an official report favoring the passport application of one "Fyodor Mikhaylovich Dostoevsky, who is under secret surveillance." The report continued: "His epileptic attacks have never before been so severe as they have been recently, especially in the past month. With each new attack his memory is more and more impaired, to such an extent that he is no longer able to recognize his closest acquaintances. Moreover, after each such attack he is seized by a melancholia and fear of death which could drive him to utter despair or madness."

This low point, however, was the crisis before that important spiritual change which dictated the whole future course of his outlook on life. The immediate cause of the transformation of Dostoevsky's *Weltanschauung* was his disappointment upon his first contact with western Europe. Formerly, he had been an adherent of Fourier's rationalistic doctrine of redemption. In the Katorga he had directly experienced the unfathomable abysses and irrationalities of human nature. Now he saw the inadequacy of a purely rationalistic system that did not take account of all aspects of the human soul.

With this taking up of new views, which he himself called "a spiritual rebirth," his creative work also veered in an entirely new direction. The first token of it in his writing is in *Notes from Underground*. This short novel is an agonized cry of protest against society by "a personality fallen under the wheel of a leveling civilization." His "underground philosopher" was the first in the procession of figures in Dostoevsky's later novels who are consistently driven by their anarchic revolt against the existing world order to destruction and self-destruction—such characters as Raskolnikov in *Crime and Punishment*, Stavrogin and Kirillov in *The Possessed*, the nihilist Hippolyte in *The Idiot*, and, finally, the finished and perfect prototype: Ivan Karamazov. The underground philosopher's monologue already contains all the elements of those intellectual dramas that reach such heights in his later work. In his keen analysis of the wildly conflicting impulses of his "hero" he first indicates his astonishingly modern insight into the human psyche. As early as this book we find Dostoevsky's relentless revelation of the moral underworld of the soul.

In the spring of 1862 he set to work on the monologue of *Notes from Underground*. But while he was writing the first draft, the novelist began on a new chapter in the turbulent novel of his life.

He met Polina Suslova in the offices of *Vremya*, and he was seized with an uncontrollable infatuation for this twenty-one-year-old student. So bitterly disappointed in marriage, he thought that this new relationship would give him compensation for all his troubles.

He decided to go to Italy with his new mistress. But the magazine's tangled affairs prevented him from leaving with Polina, so that she had to set out alone. Soon afterward he began to receive impatient letters from Paris. Polina hinted that she could not wait for him much longer. He continued to postpone his departure, and at last received the crushing news that if he came now he would be too late; during her vain wait Polina had fallen in love with a young Spanish plantation owner.

Frantic with jealousy, Dostoevsky now dropped everything; and with only enough money for his fare set out for Paris to struggle with the rival for Polina. On the train, however, he came to his senses, and realized that for the contest with this rich Spaniard he would have to have funds. The route from Petersburg to Paris passed through the German gambling and bath resorts. Dostoevsky was struck by the tempting thought that the money he needed could be won at the roulette table. In Wiesbaden he cut short his trip and went directly from the railroad station to the casino.

His stay—he had meant to stop over for only a few hours—lasted several days. At first his dream seemed to be coming true; he won and won again, and soon had all the money he thought he should need in Paris. But once he had plunged into the frenzy of gambling, he forgot what had brought him to the casino. He forgot the situation of his mistress, forgot his jealousy, forgot everything—and played on in a mental stupor. He had already lost half of his new gains when he awoke from the enchantment and, recalling his original intention, resumed his trip to Paris.

There he found Polina utterly crushed; the rich Spaniard had deserted her. Instead of romantically flinging himself into the struggle against a rival, Dostoevsky once again found himself playing the part of unselfish friend and consoler. The money he had won was soon spent. Intrigued by the success of his first try at gambling, he proposed to Polina that she and he go back to Wiesbaden so that he could win enough money for their trip to Italy.

Wiesbaden was not the end of it. When he lost there, he tried his luck in Baden-Baden. He traveled around from one casino to the next, always imbued with the "certain knowledge" that he would be able to force fortune to yield to him.

During this restless period of traveling he found neither the tranquillity nor the concentration to finish *Notes from Underground*, which he had begun with such high hopes in Petersburg. But he conceived the idea for a new novel. He decided to describe the fantastic milieu to which his unfortunate love affair had led him: the harried people who besieged the roulette table by the hundreds; the shifting expressions of these gamblers who trembled for every gulden; the greedy hands that lunged forward to gather up their winnings; and among them he himself, his experience with Polina, his reckless gamble for her, the dangerous state of mind it imposed upon him, his own avarice as he stared at the heaps of money on the green table, the pounding of his heart as he watched the rolling ball, and his trembling hands as he placed his stakes.

Once before he had described an inferno that he himself experienced, the hell of Siberian forced labor. Now he intended to do this new work as a conscious parallel to the earlier one, a portrayal of this second hell he was experiencing. "It must again be the description of a kind of steam-bath in prison, and I will make the greatest effort to describe it all in vivid pictures," he wrote of this idea for a gambling novel. On the strength of an outline of it, he hoped to get a considerable advance, enough to enable him and Polina to continue their trip to Italy.

He did get the advance on the book, but he did not get around to the writing of it. Its subject rode him like an obsession, and he could not master it; he was doomed to live out the novel which he had intended only to write. For he himself was now a gambler and the slave of the demon of chance; he was senselessly squandering all his strength and vital energies. The exhausting life of the fortune hunter left him no leisure for thinking, let alone for work. A few brief observations, half-phrases that he noted on scraps of paper during his desperate odyssey through the gaming halls, were all that the artist could wrest from the gambler.

When at last he did miraculously win enough money for the trip to Italy, the inferno of his marriage pulled him back. In Turin the runaway husband received the news that his wife's condition had taken a fatal turn for the worse. Haunted by pity and a sense of guilt, he decided to hurry back to her sickbed.

When he reached home, he found his dying, consumptive wife in a state of total psychic breakdown. Maria Dmitrievna's lust for life, hysterically intensified by her approaching end, bordered on madness.

All through the winter he was chained to the bedside of his wife as she struggled with death. While he toiled, trying to complete the *Notes from Underground*, he kept listening to her pain-ful coughing. Maria's attacks of hysteria and shortness of breath forced him again and again to interrupt his work. Then she be-came possessed by a mania for winding up clocks until the springs broke; afterward she furiously demanded that he make them go again. Or she would be terrified that there were demons in her room, and to calm her Dostoevsky had to drop his writing and chase the "demons" out of the window by waving a cloth.

"I have never been in a worse state," he wrote to his brother at the time. "The cell in the fortress, the Katorga, the barracks—all these things were shadows; the present alone is the real inferno."

Shortly afterward Maria passed away. During the vigil at the dead woman's bier Dostoevsky wrote his *Meditations on Christ*. It began as a lament: "Masha lies on the bier; shall I ever see Masha again? . . ." But then he transcended his personal grief to think of the destiny of human life and its symbolization in the figure of Christ. These notes, written in mourning, were the first formulation of his concept of a universe suffused with Christ—the concept which underlies all of his later works. It was the first testament of a new Christian faith.

Once he had finished *Notes from Underground*, he felt the life-stirrings of the great Katorga novel which had been gestating since Siberia. And so, shortly after Maria's death, he set to work on the Raskolnikov novel. All the elements for it were at hand. If only inspiration would help him hit upon the right dramatic plot, he hoped to be able to write the novel within a few weeks.

But his personal misfortunes, which again and again thwarted his creative activity, were not yet at an end. Just after Dostoevsky had drafted a preliminary character sketch of his protagonist, a new blow fell, harder and more fateful than any of the past. His brother Michael, who was to him "the most deeply loved person on earth," died.

Michael's passing, besides affecting him emotionally, had the gravest material consequences for Dostoevsky. It imposed a burden he was to bear almost to the end of his life. For Michael had left behind, as his total fortune, thirty rubles. This just about paid for his funeral. He also left an array of debts amounting to twenty-five thousand rubles. The magazine *Epocha*, which Michael had founded shortly before his death, had had to fight against great financial difficulties from the very beginning. After Michael's death not a kopek's worth of credit could be obtained for the enterprise, and yet the magazine was obligated to its subscribers to bring out at least six more issues, which would require a minimum capital of eight thousand rubles. To protect the honor of his dead brother, Dostoevsky resolved to take upon himself both these burdens, and in addition to care for Michael's widow and his three children.

As soon as the creditors had his signature they began to worry him with claims, and finally gave him just twelve days in which to settle the notes that had fallen due.

In this emergency the publisher Stellovsky, a notorious exploiter and usurer, made Dostoevsky an offer. He would pay the author three thousand rubles for the rights to all his previously published works if Dostoevsky would write a new novel for him and deliver it before November 1, 1866. If the novel were delivered as much as a day late, a special clause provided that Dostoevsky would have to pay back the advance, and, as additional penalty, surrender to Stellovsky without compensation the rights to his entire output. This applied to previously published works as well as any he might write in the future.

Stellovsky allowed him twelve days to think it over—exactly the length of the reprieve he had received from the creditors. Thus Dostoevsky's only course was to sign this contract.

Of the three thousand rubles that Stellovsky agreed to pay, Dostoevsky really received only one hundred and seventy-five. The cunning publisher had previously bought up cheaply through middlemen the major part of the notes that were due, so that, as the owner of the notes, he could claim back most of the money he had agreed to pay Dostoevsky. There were, however, a large number of notes that had not yet fallen due, and these remained in the hands of the other creditors, who came to Dostoevsky's house to dun him from morning to night.

The only chance he saw to take care of these obligations was by making a grand coup at roulette. And so, with the little money he had left, he went abroad once more. He arranged a rendezvous with Polina, his faithful gambling companion, and reached Wiesbaden at the end of July, a few weeks before she was to come. Soon after his arrival at the resort he was forced to pawn the valuables he had with him.

During the preceding months his sorrow for his deceased brother, the burden of settling the affairs of the bankrupt *Epocha*, the struggle with the creditors, and now the breathless pursuit of a grand coup, had driven out of his mind every thought of *Crime and Punishment*. Then, as he sat in despair at Wiesbaden, disappointed in all his hopes, not knowing how to pass the time until Polina's arrival—suddenly inspiration took possession of him. One "black day" he had lost so much that he was compelled to take to the pawnshop an object he especially loved. There the usurious pawnbroker, a woman, let him have only a third of its value. As he walked in deep bitterness down the boulevard, the complete plot of his novel suddenly came to him full-blown. He sent Katkov, the editor of the *Russian Messenger*, a detailed synopsis, promised to write the novel in five weeks, and pleaded for an advance of three hundred rubles.

It was now more vital than ever to go on playing until he had won at least enough to pay his hotel bill and keep himself alive until the advance came.

Every morning he was the first at the casino, and every night he was the last to leave. Ravaged by the fever of gambling, he would then return to his wretched hotel room and work through the night on his novel. Night after night the pages of the manuscript piled up. He had already written the first two chapters, but still the expected reply and the money from Katkov had not arrived, and his luck stubbornly continued to fail, so that he had to pawn his whole wardrobe piece by piece.

When Polina arrived at last at the end of August, the eagerly awaited reunion came down to a few days together in an unpaid-for, shabby hotel room. It took only that long before Polina's slender funds had been gambled away also; her belongings too were pawned and the proceeds lost at roulette, and she was left with a tiny sum, just enough for her to flee this misery and go to Paris. Dostoevsky remained behind, his predicament growing worse every day.

In all of Dostoevsky's life, rich as it was in humiliating experiences, there are few incidents that can compare with the rest of his stay at Wiesbaden. The proprietor of the hotel informed him that as long as he was not in a position to earn any money, he need not eat. Until he paid his bills he would be given no more credit; however, the hotel would go on serving him hot tea—just hot tea—twice a day.

During the first few days, in order to conceal his embarrassing situation from the other hotel guests, he would leave the hotel an hour before lunch and not return until late in the evening. But soon he noticed with alarm that these walks increased his appetite. And so—a prisoner to his lack of money—he stayed in his room for days at a time, limiting his excursions to walks to the nearest post office, where he mailed, without stamps, begging letters to his friends.

Yet in spite of all his cares, his thoughts were so filled with Raskolnikov's murder that he worked night after night on *Crime and Punishment*. But his body, weakened by hunger, soon refused to go on with this forced labor; the mere physical exertion of sitting upright for hours at his desk became increasingly hard for him.

When at last his tallow candle burned down and the hotelkeeper refused him credit for another candle, he had to stop working. By day condemned to hunger and self-enforced imprisonment in his room, by night to darkness, hunger, and inactivity, he endured the most frightful hardship, until at last the money arrived.

He had come to Wiesbaden hoping to make a grand coup that would free him from debts and cares and permit him to write undisturbed at home. Now the money he received was just enough for him to pay his hotel bill, redeem his wardrobe, and buy a ticket back to his old misery, to the same gloomy house in the poor quarter of Petersburg where he made his student Raskolnikov live. There he continued his work on *Crime and Punishment*. Meanwhile the *Russian Messenger* had already begun publishing those chapters of the novel which he had written in Wiesbaden. Therefore he was driven into a hectic race with time. He had to write a new installment every month for the next number of the magazine. To meet the deadline he had to strain his imagination, and that under the most unfavorable external conditions.

"I am living like a beggar, and am often forced to run around for three days in order to borrow a ruble somewhere. Then to sit down and write—sometimes it is a sheer impossibility," he groaned.

Crime and Punishment was supposed to be finished by winter. In frantic haste Dostoevsky was writing a new installment —the decisive interview between the detective, Porfiry Petrovitch, and the murderer, Raskolnikov. Exactly one month away, November 1, was the deadline by which time he had to deliver a new novel to Stellovsky. It was not that he had no suitable material on hand. There was his novel on gambling, for which he had many notes hurriedly scribbled on scraps of paper. The theme seemed made for the purpose. But how he hated to tear himself away from the feverish suspense of the scene between Porfiry and Raskolnikov and turn his imagination into a different channel— to sketch the fate and the mental state of a deluded gambler. Moreover, the contract stipulated that the new novel would have to have a length of at least ten signatures; Dostoevsky pondered the sheer physical impossibility of writing ten signatures in four weeks.

At this point the third woman entered his life. It was his predicament that led her to him. Friends to whom he turned in his despair advised him to get the help of a stenographer, since that at least would speed up the technical work. The head of a stenographic school gave him the name of his best pupil, twenty-year-old Anna Grigorievna Snitkin.

Dostoevsky's third love began as a prosaic work relationship. Every morning the stenographer came to his lodgings. He dictated to her what he had thought out during the night, and she transcribed her notes into a neat longhand copy. She began assisting him on the fourth of October; twenty-four days later, in large part thanks to this skillful and speedy helper, the manuscript of *The Gambler* was ready for delivery.

This should have taken care of the danger of Stellovsky. But when Dostoevsky attempted to deliver the novel on the appointed day, it developed that the publisher had taken himself off; he was trying to make doubly sure that Dostoevsky's complete works would fall into his hands. In this situation Anna Grigorievna's alertness came to Dostoevsky's aid. She deposited the finished manuscript at the police station, requesting an official receipt confirming the day and hour it had been turned in. Thus she saved Dostoevsky's work from the usurer's grasp.

The collaboration which had begun at so fateful a time continued, and in the course of four more weeks the rest of *Crime and Punishment* was also completed. Out of their successful working relationship grew friendship, and out of that, love, a love which in spite of its sober beginning led to marriage. Against the background of this marriage, which was so opportune for Dostoevsky's creative work, the undiminished harshness of his life stands out in even sharper contrast.

Crime and Punishment—Dostoevsky's first really great commercial success—coming at a time when he was living in misery, brought him fourteen thousand rubles. But what seemed a blessing was at once transformed into a curse; for as soon as the creditors scented money they got busy. They took every kopek of the money he had earned by his grueling labor; and since there wasn't enough to satisfy them all, those who received the short end of the stick threatened to have him locked up in debtor's prison if he did not meet their notes. Once before there had been a crucial change in the direction of his work which had coincided with a collapse in his outer circumstances—the shift from the romanticism of *The Insulted and Injured* to the realism of *Notes from Underground*. This latest misfortune also coincided with a new inward development, one which was again to transform his work. His underground philosopher and his Raskolnikov had symbolized the power of negative and destructive forces. But the movement of his thought was fugal, and now, out of initially chaotic sketches, there emerged a contrapuntal theme—the counterpoise to evil, the power of the positive and good, the Christ-principle in human nature.

The idea for *The Idiot* began to take shape. He was haunted by the figure of Prince Myshkin. In this forerunner of Elder Zossima and Alyosha Karamazov, the representatives of the pure in heart, purity ascends to "evangelical holiness."

But at this turning point in his creative life, he had to drop everything, and, to escape being clapped into prison, go abroad. He took with him his young wife and assistant. Although they were virtually going into exile, his mood was one of confidence. Since Anya, angelically patient and self-sacrificing, had begun helping him, he had worked better than ever before. With her near him, he would finish *The Idiot* quickly too, and its success would permit him to return to his homeland. "Only a year of peace from the creditors, and it will be easy for me to pay all my debts from the proceeds of my work," he wrote at the time.

The couple went first to Berlin. But "this horrible city" was no place for him to work. They traveled on to Dresden, but there too he did not find the peace he longed for. They went to Switzerland; they kept moving from country to country, from city to city, eternally searching for the right environment for writing. No country and no city offered the stimulus and serenity he longed for. Being abroad was to blame for it; this enforced banishment, these foreign lands, stood in the way of his work. He simply could not get accustomed to "this world outside Russia." "Really, why am I in Dresden?" he asked. "But no matter where I am, in this city or that, no matter where, I feel like a slice of bread that has been severed from the loaf." And when adverse circumstances kept him for some time in Florence, he wrote: "When I see all the Englishmen and Frenchmen in the streets here, I cannot understand why these people who have money to leave remain in this hell of their own free will." In every one of his letters of that period he expresses the pain of being uprooted; again and again the same outcry breaks forth: "I need home in order to be able really to work again. I feel that without the Russian earth all my strength, all my talent will dry up."

The slender advances he received from Russia were just enough for him to eke out a bare existence abroad, and his poverty magnified the misery of being cut off from home. True, by flight he had succeeded in escaping his creditors, but he had run into another breed of persecutors—hotelkeepers who presented him with overdue bills, landladies who threatened to call the police, shopkeepers who refused him credit, pawnbrokers who looked him over suspiciously. For him Germans, Swiss, and Italians could be lumped together as a single pack of tormentors; all the streets of foreign lands became ugly alleys that led to the pawnshop.

Since his youth he had suffered from epilepsy, and all his writing had been done with the specter of illness at his back. But in his exile the disease struck with greater force than ever before. Almost as soon as he left Russia, the frequency of the attacks began to increase; they occurred weekly, in fact often only days apart, two or three times in succession. He would just have rolled his cigarette and written down the first few sentences, when he would be overcome by a feeling as though his soul were plunging into bottomless depths. He felt seized by the awe of annihilation; an inarticulate cry would be wrenched from his throat; his face would contort; and he would fall unconscious from his chair. "A little death," he called this condition; and often, so closely did the disease simulate approaching death, he would take leave of his wife like a dying man. After every attack he was so shattered that he would lie all day in a stupor, scarcely speaking, and unable to gather his thoughts together. If he afterward forced himself to work, he noticed with horror that he had lost his memory, and frequently could not even recall the names of his heroes. Often these postepileptic twilight states lasted more than a week.

Day after day, night after night, he put his mind to the severest test, and yet after weeks of labor he had got together scarcely more than a crude draft of *The Idiot*. Europe was worse than the Katorga.

Under these dismal conditions, the hopes he had placed in his novel melted away to nothing. His work would never make possible the longed-for return to Russia. Only a grand coup at roulette could give him the money he needed; only large winnings would free him at one stroke from these unbearable foreign lands and from the threat of debtors' prison in Russia. If he won, he won his life, his work, everything. All he needed was a run of luck in order to be free, free of all cares forever. In his insoluble predicament he must try it at least once more; he owed it to his work, to his dead brother's family, to Anya, and to his own future.

Pure reason advised him to take this step. But pure reason has its sophistries; in this case it was in league with his lurking passion. The hope of winning a return to Russia at roulette may well have been the immediate pretext that brought him to the casino again; but what held him there afterward was the irresistible attraction of gambling itself. For once he had begun, it did not matter whether he won or lost; every incident, every circumstance at the gaming table served him equally as a fresh stimulus to go on gambling. If he won, his winning was a sign to go on; if he lost, he could not rest until he had won back his losses. "The principal thing is the game itself," he confessed.

To his three afflictions—exile, poverty, and illness—there was added a fourth: the obsessive passion for gambling that had its source in the depths of his own nature. It was this that completed the doom of his life in exile.

As in a Greek tragedy, from then on all evil hazards intertwined, all the conflicts mounted inexorably toward disaster. As though the hostile goddess of fate, Ate, were punishing him for the *hybris* with which he attempted to bend fortune to his will, his pursuit of a coup at roulette carried him headlong to destruction.

For small as were the advances and loans that he received from Russia, they had at least assured him a frugal living. But now, when he staked his whole existence on the hazard of the gaming table, even this meager security vanished. Obsessed by the delusion that every tiny stake could bring him the large winnings he needed, he wagered his last penny at roulette. But the salvation that he hoped for again and again proved to be an illusion that led him toward a profounder wretchedness than he had ever before experienced.

In the winter of 1867, in Geneva, he and his wife did not have so much as five francs—and obtained that sum only by luckily meeting a Russian acquaintance in the street. "Had it not been for that chance, we should have died of hunger in this foreign city," he wrote home. Since he had no money for fuel, he had to work on his novel at temperatures of more than ten degrees Fahrenheit below freezing. Later, when his first, eagerly awaited child, his daughter Sonya, came into the world, he possessed a total of seventy francs, of which forty had to be paid to the nurse at once. Even with the most careful budgeting the remainder would last no more than six days. Shortly afterward the infant sickened and died, and the grief-stricken father had tht greatest difficulty raising money for the burial.

In Dresden, where Anya gave birth to their second child, the family found itself in an even more wretched situation. An installment of seventy-five rubles on an advance Dostoevsky was expecting from Kaspirevitch, the editor of the magazine *Zaria*, for *The Eternal Husband*, had not arrived. Dostoevsky visited the bank every day, to ask at the window in a trembling voice whether the money had arrived. The clerks got into the habit of making fun of him on account of his repeated vain inquiries. "If you only knew," he wrote to a friend, "in what a position we are, I, my wife who is nursing a child and must eat well, and the child, which may fall ill because of our penury. We must have her baptized, but have not yet done so for lack of funds. Does Kaspirevitch think that the letter in which I described my destitute condition was a literary exercise and nothing more? How can I work when I am hungry and have had to pawn my very breeches to get the two thalers for the telegram. The devil take me and my hunger. But she, my wife, who is now suckling her infant, she had to go to the pawnshop herself and pledge her last warm coat. And it is already snowing here. . . . If you only knew under what tortures I have to work."

When the expected money arrived at last, it was instantly spent to settle the most urgent bills. Meanwhile Dostoevsky had finished the manuscript, but he had no money to mail it: "It is heavy, and the postage amounts to five thalers. And after all, we must have something to live on. Oh, how rotten everything is."

Going out of the gambling casino in Hamburg he had a severe epileptic fit. He fell on the pavement and injured himself. He returned to Dresden "like a whipped dog," to resume his interrupted labors on *The Possessed*.

It was not enough that the passion for gambling stole the last gulden out of his pocket, the ring from his finger, the clothes from his body; it also robbed him of the one property he still possessed: the little time that remained for working, the hours he did not spend trying to raise a ruble or to recover from an attack of epilepsy.

During his former stay at Wiesbaden he had at least had the strength to wrest something from his slavery to the roulette table: he used the nights for his work. But now he had wholly abandoned himself to the gambling passion, and was the prey of his vice by night as well as by day. After his constant losses the idea occurred to him to beat the game by ingenious mathematical calculations. And so now, when the casino closed after midnight and he returned to his hotel room, he did not take up the unfinished manuscript, but turned to the notes he had made during the play on the recurrence of certain numbers and colors. He would work until dawn on an "infallible" system. Gambling even gained dominion over the few hours of sleep he allowed himself, for then, as he reported, he went on calculating in his dreams.

In brief sane moments of self-criticism he realized with horror the material and moral ruin into which his passion was plunging him. This time it was not Polina, the light-minded mistress and adventurous fellow gambler, whom he was dragging down into his own misery, but an innocent young creature, his wedded wife, Anya. "Support and consolation," he called her, and his "guardian angel." And what was he doing? He left Anya to rely on the kindness of some casual German landlady and went off to roulette. "How could I desert such a dear angel who so quietly trusts me? Why am I away from you; where is this journey taking me?" he laments in a spell of penitence. "I know that with such characterless, useless behavior I am endangering you. It is terribly stupid of me, mean. But there is a tiny chance. . . ." And in the end this tiny chance would always win out over all insight and regret.

On this occasion he had promised Anya to be back with her in two days. A week passed. And Anya was not merely his patient wife, but his literary collaborator. She had become a part of his creative life. While she now waited despairingly for him, his work also waited.

"I know I have ruined your life, but forgive me and save me just this once more," he implored her. "I am in a desperate predicament and cannot come back. Send me the money just for the fare." But after he had received the money, he wrote in self-abasement: "I have committed a crime. I have gambled away everything, everything. Send me money just this once more, even if it is the last you have."

Anya pawned her earrings to send him the money. He swore to himself to play just once more in order to redeem the jewels with his winnings. But on the very next day he accused himself: "I am worse than a dog, Anya. Last night I won a considerable sum; today I have not a kopek left." Anya had to take her wedding ring to the pawnshop. Utterly crushed, he came home the following night, threw himself sobbing at her feet, and implored her to trust him just this once more. But the following morning he secretly removed her last possessions from her wardrobe and pawned them. Anya was ill, Anya was nursing her child. But an irresistible compulsion overcame him; he began placing bets in his mind, and imagining what was happening in the gambling room. He was no longer master of himself. Leaving Anya behind, he went to the casino.

He had already passed through many an inferno; but this moral hell into which he was driven by his "cursed vice" and his "all too passionate nature" was worse than anything else. Tormented by shame and repentance, he resolved again and again to leave off gambling, that "diabolical possession, that self-poisoning" by his own imagination, and to live at Anya's side for his work alone. "I shall have only the one goal in view: to finish the novel swiftly and successfully. I will put my whole soul into the work. If it succeeds, we are saved."

But he could not escape. He would sit at his desk struggling to portray a pure man in the image of Christ—his Prince Myshkin —and then the polluted dream of gambling would break in. Once more he outlined the "main idea" of his whole life: the purification of the "great sinner" in God; he conceived those moving dialogues in *The Possessed* that touch upon the ultimate meaning of existence—and he was condemned to stop his work for days, even weeks, to lead the empty existence of a professional gambler. The mind that created immortal characters frittered away night after night in ridiculous calculations. And the hand that wrote great dialogues on the being or nonbeing of God laid down the pen to force its shaky way among the avaricious hands of the casino mob and stake a last thaler.

Superb scenes that the creative artist sketched at his desk, and wretched scenes that made up the life of the gambler; exaltation of the mind, and humiliation by vice; the noblest of truths in his manuscripts, and the shabbiest lies in begging letter to his wife; worry about a convincing portrayal of Stavrogin, and worry about a few extra thalers that he must somehow persuade the pawnbroker to let him have—all these contradictions were inextricably confused during this period. The mountain path to artistic perfection and the way through the morass of passion ran parallel, side by side.

For years this tragic struggle lasted. It was not until he suffered devastating losses in 1871 in Wiesbaden that he was finally cured and at last able to write jubilantly: "Anya, a wonderful thing has happened to me: the hideous illusion that has tormented me for almost ten years is gone. Ten years, ever since the death of my brother, under the crushing pressure of debts, I have dreamed of gambling, constantly, earnestly, passionately; but now all that is over; this was the very last time. Do you believe, Anya, that my hands are now free? I was bound by gambling; now I will think of nothing but work."

Without regard to possible consequences, he decided in June, 1871, to return to Russia. It was not until the last minute that he received the sum he needed, and now at last he had the strength of mind not to gamble the money away.

Free of the agony of exile, and purged of his gambling compulsion, Dostoevsky's last decade began after his return home. It was the decade of his rise. The energy and efficiency of his "guardian angel" saved him from the imprisonment that threatened in Russia. Anya now took over his financial affairs, conducted the struggle with his creditors, and adroitly worked out compromises.

In those last ten years Dostoevsky finished *The Possessed*, wrote two of his finest tales, *A Gentle Spirit* and *The Dream of a Ridiculous Man*, composed his last great novels, *A Raw Youth* and *The Brothers Karamazov*, and began publishing *The Diary of a Writer*, which appeared periodically. *The Brothers Karamazov*, which was published serially, and the political essays in *The Diary of a Writer* made him the spiritual counselor of his nation.

Half a year before his death he delivered his historic address on the occasion of the Pushkin celebration in Moscow. This address was his political testament. The enthusiastic audience paid him such homage as no literary artist and no statesman in Russia had ever before received. Intoxicated by his speech, strangers embraced one another; and lifelong enemies were reconciled and promised henceforth to love one another. For a second time he heard the words that had greeted him at the beginning of his career: "You are a genius, a genius." This time they came from the lips of his bitter foe, Turgenev, who was so overwhelmed by Dostoevsky's address that he rushed up to him, kissed him, and congratulated him.

But even as at the beginning of his career, when success and fame came they were the briefest flickers of triumph in the over-all tragedy of this artist's life. Even at the summit of his fame, Dostoevsky went on with his work in the teeth of illness and financial troubles. He endured severe attacks of epilepsy while working on his last two novels, and he noted the effect of these upon his constitution. "My work progresses very slowly. I am afraid the falling sickness has robbed me not only of my memory, but also of my imagination. . . . I do not know whether this time my strength and health will hold out under the kind of convict labor I have hitherto imposed upon myself."

This man, who at the Pushkin celebration had been lauded as the greatest of writers and the "prophet of the nation," wrote: "Now the time has come when I must finish *The Brothers Karamazov* without delay and draw up the accounting in this work. It is personally dear to me, for I have put much of my own self into it. But . . . I am working nervously, amid torments and cares. . . . Only a few passages that were dictated to me directly by my imagination have been successful at first draft; everything else has been hard work."

In bed after a lung hemorrhage on January 25, from which he died two days later, he reached for his pen once more. But it was only to write one of those numerous pleas which make up the largest part of the seven hundred of his letters that have been preserved. Thus the last piece of writing from Dostoevsky's hand was addressed to his publisher, Katkov. It reads: "May I ask once more in this, perhaps my *last request*, for your courtesy and aid? According to your accounting, somewhat more than four thousand rubles are coming to me. At the present moment I am in great need of money. Please see to it that it is paid out to me at once. You do not know how much you will oblige me by doing this; right now it is extremely urgent for me to obtain this sum."

CHAPTER THREE

SUBLIMATION THROUGH ART

PARADOX, instead of comprehensible laws, seemed to rule all the events in Dostoevsky's life; and that same paradox dominated the process of his artistic creation. Strange as it may seem, the distress and hardships that were imposed upon Dostoevsky the man turned out to be blessings for his literary activity. Every blow of fate was a fresh stimulus to the artist within him; every outward loss was an inner gain. The gargoyle faces that maliciously presided over his day-to-day existence were made over in the world of his art into the angelic countenances of guardian spirits.

He stood before the firing squad and faced death. But for Dostoevsky those minutes of imminent death became the deepest and most fruitful experience. They changed fundamentally his attitude toward life, and made him aware of the full preciousness of simple existence. "Why, if ever I could return to life again," the thought flashed through his mind during that last minute, "what an eternity of days! And all would be mine. How I would preserve and cherish every minute in order not to miss a single one."

The affirmation of life that bursts forth again and again amid the horrors in his books was born out of his encounter with death. It is the same joyful affirmation we see in his pure Fool, Prince Myshkin, to whom the author assigns the tale of his own experience on the scaffold. That feeling leads Myshkin to cry out in childlike amazement: "I do not understand how anyone can pass by a tree without being happy that it is. . . . How many wonderful things everyone meets with every step through life."

This affirmation of life also inspires Elder Zossima's religious message: that above all we must learn to love life; that is the prerequisite for a revelation of God's secret will in all things. The dying Stepan Trofimovitch in *The Possessed,* the candidate for suicide in *The Dream of a Ridiculous Man,* and even the cynical cellar philosopher of *Notes from Underground,* the innocent Dmitri in chains and the atheist Ivan Karamazov—all are filled with this love for life. And in the last scene of *The Brothers Karamazov* this affirmation is once more triumphantly voiced by Alyosha, the prophet of future man.

It was only this positive attitude toward life that gave Dostoevsky the strength to turn those "four horrible years" at forced labor to his spiritual advantage as both man and artist. "Many a time I blessed destiny for this experience," he wrote later. "I cannot at all say what a transformation my soul, my faith, my mind underwent during those four years. . . . Without it, my strict review of my life would never have taken place." The Katorga led him back to faith. "In the forlornness of forced labor, one thirsts for faith like dry grass for the rain and one finds it at last only because the truth is seen more clearly in time of misfortune." His faith, acquired in misfortune and purified by pain, is basic to all his feelings. From it he derived his compassionate love for those who, "arrested in guilt and afflictions, are more deserving of love than the guiltless and the fortunate. . . ."

Later, when someone remarked that his exile had been an injustice, he objected: "Perhaps the Almighty had to send me there, so that I could learn the essence of things in order to communicate it to others."

When Oscar Wilde returned to the world after two years in Reading Gaol, the artist in him was almost extinguished; for a while afterward what was but a living corpse haunted the Paris boulevard cafés under the borrowed name of the satanic wanderer Sebastian Malmoth. For Dostoevsky prison was a tremendous experience; those four years of forced labor in Siberia brought out the creative artist in him.

In Dostoevsky's later life of freedom, poverty brought ample sufferings and humiliations, which again opened his eyes to the many shapes that shame takes for the needy, to the vast painful drama of human misery. The many poor and insulted characters in his novels wear the threadbare dress of his own poverty, and help him bear the burden of his own insults. It is the personal knowledge of suffering that speaks so movingly, so powerfully, and with such living directness out of his books.

There was, however, something that caused him more suffering than the pangs of poverty and the ordeals of the Katorga. This was his "exile" in foreign countries. Yet this frustration was also to fructify his creative life. His never-ending troubles abroad helped to form his negative picture of Europe; his constant, consuming longing for home created in his mind the positive counterpart to Europe—a mystically transfigured Russia.

Since every tension, every stimulus to his temperament was sublimated in art, the agitation of the gaming casino also was not without profit to his work. It too was channelized into impulses and forces for creation. Coming straight from a contest at the gaming table, still shaking with inner turbulence, he gave birth, as if in convulsive labor, to some of the most tremendous scenes and characters in his novels. It was almost as if his nerves, "which could only be stimulated, but never satiated," demanded this recurrent emotional flagellation.

With some artists the creative process is finally and completely choked out by sickness. Dostoevsky, however, not only overcame the curse of his disease, but forced it to serve his art. A shuddering plunge of the mind into impotence and darkness— that was the epileptic attack. But in the last seconds of consciousness before it (his Prince Myshkin and Kirillov have described the author's own experience of the course of an epileptic fit) "all the forces of life gathered convulsively all at once into the highest attainable consciousness. The sensation of life, of being, multiplied tenfold at that moment; all passion, all doubt, all unrest were resolved as in a higher peace, in a peace full of clear, harmonious joy and hope. And then it seemed suddenly as if something were opening up in the soul; an indescribable, an unknown light radiated, by which the ultimate essence of things was made visible and recognizable. . . . All this lasted at most a second, possibly the same during which Mohammed's pitcher, filled to the brim, overturned and yet did not have time to spill, while in the same second Mohammed gazed upon all the gardens of Allah."

When Dostoevsky considered these attacks in retrospect, like his epileptic heroes he had to admit that these light-phenomena and moments of higher consciousness were merely a part of his affliction. And nevertheless he concluded: "What does it matter if it is a disease? What do I care whether it is normal or not normal, if in retrospect and in a healthy state I still feel that moment as one of perfect harmony and beauty, and if it arouses in me hitherto unsuspected emotions, gives me feelings of magnificence, abundance, and eternity, and reconciles me to everyone—if it is like a glorious, heavenly merging with the highest synthesis of life."

The unrest preceding attacks, to which he owed his most intense psychic experiences and visions, decisively influenced his whole creative life. From attack to attack he recognized with increasing distinctness that his best periods of literary production coincided with this epileptic "aura," the "prodromal state." In order to trace the peculiar functional relationship between his writing and his disease, he began to keep regular diary records of his attacks, putting the entries side by side with his literary notes.

Since even the agony of his epilepsy contributed to his art, he at last came to look upon it as a grim gift of God. He called it his "holy disease." "You healthy people," he once said, "have no conception of the glorious ecstasy that permeates the epileptic before the attack. I do not know whether this rapture lasts for hours or seconds, but believe me, I would not exchange it for all the joys of life. I would be prepared to give my whole life for it."

Dostoevsky's inner life, like his outer existence, was always imperiled and on the verge of destruction. His light was wrested from the darkness, his ethics "from a chaos at whose bottom seethed all the passions of human nature." His goal was the summit of the human mind; yet to reach that, he had to wade through the low-lying swamps of the instincts. He took up the burden of undeserved suffering, and added to it the weight of the griefs he himself was to blame for. From his comprehensive self-understanding he created the "all too comprehensive" nature of the Karamazovs, which was "capable of embracing the two opposed infinities: the infinity of the radiant ideals above us and the infinity of the darkest degradation beneath us." His own mind was "the battleground where God and the Devil strive for mastery," and the issue of his inner battle determined his life.

In his harrowing self-analysis, and in the ruthless exposition of what analysis uncovered, Dostoevsky resembles St. Augustine —the first of the great "confessors." It was as though Dostoevsky went down into the caves of his heart and explored the farthermost tunnels and hiding places of this moral underworld. Anguished by religious scruples, his testimony against himself was harsher than anything a hostile witness could charge. In his contrition he accused himself more mercilessly than could any prosecutor. Thirsting for religious purification, he judged himself more sternly than any earthly court. For he tried himself by the code of the Last Judgment: the shadow of a sinful thought was enough for a verdict of "Guilty."

Dostoevsky's preoccupation with his own sinfulness and his religious scruples were shared by his two great contemporaries in Russian literature: Gogol and Tolstoy.

Gogol, in the throes of a moral crisis, looked into himself and saw the evil that was inside him. At once the artist in him turned to stone, as at the sight of the Gorgon. Horrified, he discovered that the vileness of Shlestakov and Chichikov, those two "devils" of his *Dead Souls,* dwelt within his own soul. Everything he had written now appeared to him as satanic projection of his own corruption. Deeply repentant, hoping to flee from his sinful self, he pledged himself to describe only goodness and purity. But what happened now was like what happened to the Russian painter Vrubel, who set out to paint Christ and in the end had painted the portrait of his own demon.

The spontaneity of Gogol's inspiration failed him when he attempted to treat virtue. A "horrible numbness" overcame him; he was no longer able to write. He interpreted these symptoms as punishment for his lifelong sinfulness. To appease God's wrath Gogol decided to sacrifice to Him his literary creations. On the night of February 11, 1852, he stalked through his rooms, carrying a burning candle and muttering prayers. At last he stopped before the fireplace and threw into the leaping flames the entire manuscript of the second part of *Dead Souls*. After having made this symbolic sacrifice, Gogol became a gloomy penitent, gnawed by anxiety. He never found release, and died deranged.

Some forty years later we see a similar tussle between Tolstoy the artist and Tolstoy the sinner, determined to cleanse himself. And in this case also the artist could not endure the guilty knowledge of the underworld of his ego. "Confronted with all the secret nastiness" of his own soul, suffering "infernal torments," the author of *War and Peace* and *Anna Karenina* renounced art as vanity; he condemned it for "obscuring the good and exposing only the ugly."

Periodically Tolstoy tried, as he put it, to sweep out the dirt that soiled his soul. Each new attempt widened the gap between the moralist and the artist in him. The penitent "sinner" who hoped to find atonement in an evangelical life dropped writing to teach at a village school. He read the lives of the saints to peasants, and took to dressing like a muzhik and going on pilgrimage to sectarians. "In a peasant smock and dirty wool socks, he sat with the peasant Mitrofan, sewing shoes for the peasant woman Agraffia."

For a whole decade the artist in him struggled with the preacher. Would this count in the peasant's blouse take up his pen, or labor with the shoemaker's awl? During those years the writer wrung from the cobbler the magnificent *Death of Ivan Ilyitch* and *The Power of Darkness*. But didacticism more and more overpowered his creative urge. In vain his wife pleaded with him "to write again in a poetical vein. . . . This is the real kind of work for which you were made," she wrote, "and outside of this sphere there is no peace for your soul." In vain Turgenev on his deathbed, writing to Tolstoy for the last time, urged the apostate: "Return to literary activity; that is your true mission; great writer of our Russian land, heed my request." There are portions of *Resurrection* which are sheer art, but this book was the swan song of Tolstoy the novelist; in the last years of his life he wanted to write nothing but tracts.

But though he had renounced the "sinful profession of writer," Tolstoy found that the realities of his life as an aristocrat always interfered with the pursuit of evangelical purity. Fleeing from home in his old age in the hope that he might spend the rest of his days in meditation, he was struck down by his last illness. He died in the stationmaster's house at the railroad station of Astapovo.

The abyss that "the great sinner" looked into was darker than these; Dostoevsky's repentance was no less genuine, his longing for purification no less passionate. But in contrast to Gogol and Tolstoy, Dostoevsky came to terms with his own lower depths. The horrors within him, and his repentance, were integrated into his art.

The Perseus myth deals with a hero who endures the sight of the Medusa, conquers her, and carries her severed head in a magic sack to the upper world, where he gives it to Athena, the mind-born goddess of art, for the adornment of her cuirass. Dostoevsky, too, descending into the underworld of his soul, slew the monster there, brought the trophy back to the upper world in the magic sack of literature, and used it for the adornment of the goddess of art. From the blood of the Gorgon sprang Pegasus, the winged horse, who with a blow of his hoof struck open the well of poetic inspiration on Mount Helicon. So, too, Dostoevsky's Pegasus sprang from the blood of Evil. It took a stroke from the hoof of this beast before the spring of Dostoevsky's inspiration gushed forth.

If we imagine his art without the evil he discovered within himself, all its marvel vanishes, and the marvel of his moral sublimation as well. For in contrast to Gogol and Tolstoy, who saw their art as a hindrance to purity and therefore believed it had to be given up, Dostoevsky realized that his art gave him his only chance for catharsis.

By his subtle psychological methods, he obtained the deeply hidden factor of evil from his soul, submitting it to repentance. He had the artist's power to give bodily form to the formless phantoms of evil, to make the gibbering demons speak, to drag into the light the horrible figure of the deed that had lain concealed behind the flimsy impulse. He could turn the frightful possibility into actual happening. By his extraordinary imaginative gift he was able to project in the clearest manner the inchoate quality of the self. With his artist's clairvoyance he could see beyond the "vortex of the ego" and view his own humanity in the light of eternal truth. Thus he discovered in evil the full meaning of defection from God; he comprehended the gravity of sin and the necessity for conversion. For Dostoevsky, the art of writing was in the truest sense of Ibsen's phrase "a sitting in judgment upon the self."

As a boy he had hated his tyrant of a father, whose alcoholism had cost him his post as hospital physician. The embittered father continually abused his children and his subordinates. At about the time the natural revolt of the suppressed son was threatening to break out, this father was murdered by his serfs. From then on Dostoevsky suffered intensely from guilty recollections of the hatred and unconscious death wishes he had harbored against his father.

The artist in him turned this vague guilt feeling into the wonderful trial scene in *The Brothers Karamazov*. His secret guilt for the murder of his father is symbolized by the brothers' complicity in Smerdyakov's murder of old Karamazov. Mitya's rage and passionate rebellion against his father would have made him quite capable of the crime, and therefore he willingly accepts as condign the punishment that judicial error has meted out. Ivan, whose intellect committed the crime in thought, undergoes the penalty of the mind—that is, disintegration in madness. In the process of artistic shaping, Dostoevsky converted his obscure guilt-feeling into that lofty ethical insight: that we do not kill only when we actually destroy someone's life. Our most secret hatreds and unconscious desires make murderers of us.

Dostoevsky the artist gives away in Raskolnikov's crime the secret thought that seized hold of Dostoevsky the gambler when he was roughly dismissed by the woman pawnbroker in Wiesbaden. At Raskolnikov's interrogation he cross-questioned his own heart and convicted it; in Raskolnikov's punishment he punished himself for his own mental guilt.

The erotic desire that once took hold of him at the sight of a young girl was transferred by a conscience ever at the service of his art to the revolting figures of Svidrigailov and Stavrogin, in whom the forbidden wish became the actual crime of rape. He condemns himself by assigning these characters to suicide.

Sigmund Freud, in his psychoanalytic essay on Dostoevsky, stated that the novelist's fondness for the portrayal of criminals and his amazing insight into the nature of crime "proves that the author identified himself with them on the basis of similar impulses." For this reason Freud felt it valid to "count Dostoevsky among the criminals." André Gide, who knows from his own work how complex is the artist's manipulation of experience, comes closer to the truth in his explanation of Dostoevsky's "criminal nature." In his sympathetic interpretation he writes: "Dostoevsky did not portray himself in Svidrigailov and Stavrogin, but rather what he might have become if he had not become himself."

By translating the latent evil within himself into drama, Dostoevsky exorcised it, and by molding his evil and vicious tendencies into characters who had names and destinies of their own, he was disassociating himself from them. Thus the artist actually saved the man, whose foremost concern was the salvation of his soul. Both artist and man emerged purified and strengthened from the journey through the morasses of Dostoevsky's soul.

Merechkovsky stated it well when he wrote: "No matter what I should hear of evil, shamefulness or even criminality in

Dostoevsky's life and actions, even if it could all be actually proved, his image would not thereby be darkened for me; the halo around his head would not be dulled, for I know that within him the blazing fire of art cleansed and refined everything."

The force of creativity within Dostoevsky stood up to all the adverse powers of the outside world during his life. It also overcame the inner foe. His art triumphed over poverty, humiliation, and disease, but its greatest victory was moral. His art helped him to escape the abyss of his own soul, where his underground ego brooded on destruction. It saved him from the madness that was the fate of his hero in *The Double,* the tragic buffoon who split into Goldyakin I and Goldyakin II. By the spell of his art he escaped the web that "the spider of sensuality" had woven around the hearts of old Karamazov and Svidrigailov.

Thanks to the sublimation of art, his dualism, the eternally contradictory impulses which are the downfall of the ambivalent heroes of his novels, was not fatal for him. Dualism was the moral tragedy for Versilov in *A Raw Youth,* who "in the same moment that he perceived everything wonderful and noble" was capable "not only of thinking the most repulsive things, but of doing them as well." And it brought the torments of schizophrenia to Mitya Karamazov, for all his aspiration toward higher things. "Eternally torn between the ideal of Sodom and the ideal of the Madonna," he cries out in helpless despair, "into what have I sunk—shame or the light? What a fearful mystery is man after all."

A number of Dostoevsky's notebooks containing sketches for *The Idiot* have been preserved. They show that the hero was initially conceived as a successor to the brutal, destructive man of the underground. We can trace the novelist's struggle with his material as he strove to mold this figure into the selfless Prince Myshkin. The same metamorphosis went on in the "underground man" within Dostoevsky himself. He portrayed the end product of that process in the purity of Prince Myshkin and Alyosha Karamazov. They are the embodiment of his ideal. His penitent heroes follow the way of the cross. Their road paralleled the progress of his own conscience from agony to expiation. In the wisdom of his Elder Zossima he records what he had learned by grace in the midst of many troubles and temptations. The Elder's view of life was essentially the view that Dostoevsky ultimately stood for, both as man and as novelist.

CHAPTER FOUR

THROUGH THE PURGATORY OF
DOUBT TO FAITH

"WHAT!" Belinsky exclaimed after a six-hour discussion with Turgenev. "We still don't know whether God exists, and you want to go to dinner!"

The question of God's existence was for Dostoevsky "the principal question that, consciously or unconsciously, I have wrestled with all my life." His whole being passionately posed this question; only the answer to it, it seemed to him, would explain the meaning of all the incomprehensible factors in life.

As the son of Michael Andreyevitch, staff physician in a hospital for the poor, Dostoevsky was born into an environment where inexplicable suffering was the common lot. His first impressions were of their poor and gloomy flat in the hospital, and of the garden bounded by the high hospital wall where the sick took the air. The first accounts he heard of what other people's lives were like were the stories the patients exchanged, tragic, tired chronicles of sickness and poverty and undeserved suffering. The question, "Is there a God?" was impressed upon him early in his boyhood.

When Dostoevsky was eight years old and serving as an acolyte in the church, he read the Book of Job, the story of the drama between God and man. "There was a man in the land of Uz, . . ." he read, whom God delivered over to the Evil One to test him; a man upon whom all possible sufferings were laden to make him rebel against the Lord. But in the end Job bowed humbly before the wisdom and omnipotence of God. For the afflicted Dostoevsky, this book was to be a guide and gospel all his life. In 1875 he wrote to his wife from the sanatorium at Ems, where he had gone for relief from his epilepsy: "I am reading the Book of Job, and it has aroused in me an almost morbid ecstasy. I put the book aside and pace back and forth for hours on end, scarcely able to keep back my tears. This book, Anya—how strange, isn't it?—was one of the first to take hold of me for life."

In his works Dostoevsky re-enacted the drama of Job, the contestants being God and the enlightened man of the nineteenth century. In addition to all the outer plagues with which Satan afflicted the Scriptural Job, the devil torments modern man by suspending him midway between belief and disbelief in God. The devil acknowledges his responsibility for this refinement of torture when he speaks mockingly to Ivan Karamazov: "Hesitation, suspense, conflict between belief and disbelief—is sometimes such torture to a conscientious man, such as you are, that it's better to hang oneself at once. Because I know it, I lead you to belief and disbelief by turns."

In the famous dialogue between Ivan and the devil, the devil candidly owns up to his diabolic intentions, and recalls his attempt to make Job rebel against God: "I fulfill my destiny, though it's against the grain—that is, to ruin thousands for the sake of saving one. How many souls have had to be ruined and how many honorable reputations destroyed for the sake of that one righteous man, Job, over whom they made such a fool of me in the old days."

The enigma of undeserved suffering, which was the Biblical Satan's trump card in his attempt to incite Job to rebellion against God, is also the trump card of the demon of doubt who spurs Dostoevsky's characters to similar revolt. The child of a socially minded age, Dostoevsky equated Job the individual with the whole of suffering humanity. And it is his humanitarianism, his social compassion, which shakes his heroes' belief in a God who can allow so much unjust suffering in the world. Horror at undeserved pain made Dostoevsky himself doubt the existence of God, so that for a time he allied himself with atheists like Belinsky who were under the sway of western European enlightenment.

In one of his prison letters he takes up the question of his doubts. The letter, addressed to the wife of the Dekabrist, N. D. Fonvizin, marks the beginning of his religious conversion: "I want to tell you this about myself: I am a child of this age, a child of disbelief and doubt, and it is probable—in fact, I know it is so—that I shall remain one to the end of my life. I have been and still am horribly tormented by longing for belief, which grows all the stronger the more reasons I have not to believe."

The agony of this alternation between the desire for belief and the bitterness of disbelief makes the atheist Kirillov in *The Possessed* cry out: "God is necessary and so must exist. . . . But I know he doesn't and can't. Surely you must understand that a man with two such ideas can't go on living."

By writing, Dostoevsky hoped to free himself from "the extreme torments of an ego torn between belief and disbelief." He originally planned his vast autobiographical cycle, *The Life of a Great Sinner,* as a "parable of atheism." His indecisive hero was, like the author himself, to reach faith only through the struggle with doubt.

"My Hosanna has passed through the purgatory of doubt and been purified by the cup of temptation," he said shortly before his death in *The Diary of a Writer.* By then he had become one of the most eloquent defenders of the established faith. His works, which proclaim that Hosanna with triumphal might, describe with equal power the purgatory of doubt which he had traversed. In the brooding soliloquies of his divided heroes he anatomized his own dilemma; their dialectics and debates are the debates that went on between the believer and the doubter within himself. In order to harden himself in his belief, he subjected it to the most severe test by going over all the arguments that had once made him doubt. Against the persuasiveness of his believers he pitted the full eloquence of his atheists.

His own pity for the innocent sufferings of humanity is reflected in Kirillov in *The Possessed.* Dostoevsky's humanitarianism, distorted into doubt, is for this religious fanatic of an atheist the chief point in his blasphemous revolt against God, who "gives life only to fill it with pain and terror, Who has created a world and left it to the play of blind chance, a vaudeville of demons and devils."

In *The Brothers Karamazov* Dostoevsky showed the drama between God and man at its climax. Here belief and disbelief clash most violently. Ivan Karamazov has been equipped with the author's own keenness of intellect. Ivan puts forward all the arguments of doubt, all of Dostoevsky's one-time objections to a divinely created universe, in the most cogent and convincing form.

"These idiots," Dostoevsky retorted irritably to the attacks of atheists who accused him of a naïve and reactionary faith, "these idiots cannot dream of doubts as grim as those that have shaken me. Nowhere in Europe (in atheistic Europe) have I found anyone who expressed the impact of doubt as I've made my Ivan do in *The Brothers Karamazov*."

"As for me," the doubter Ivan says to his religious brother Alyosha, "I've long resolved not to think whether man created God or God man. . . . And therefore I tell you that I accept God simply, and what's more I accept His wisdom, His purpose— which are utterly beyond our ken; I believe in the underlying order and the meaning of life; I believe in the eternal harmony in which they say we shall one day be blended. . . . It's not that I don't accept God, you must understand, it's the world created by Him that I don't and cannot accept. . . . I say nothing of the sufferings of grown-up people; they have eaten the apple, damn them, and the devil take them all. I want to speak only of the children. . . . Of the tears of humanity with which the earth is soaked from its crust to its center, I will say nothing. . . . But these, these. . . . Can you understand why a little creature, who can't even understand what's done to her, should beat her little aching heart with her tiny fists in the dark and the cold, and weep her meek, unresentful tears to dear, kind God to protect her? . . . If all must suffer to pay for the eternal harmony, what have children to do with it? And if it is really true that they must share responsibility for the father's crimes, such a truth is not of this world and is beyond my comprehension. . . . Oh, Alyosha, I am not blaspheming! I understand, of course, what an upheaval of the universe it will be when everything in heaven and earth blends in one hymn of praise, and everything that lives and has lived cries aloud: 'Thou art just, O Lord.' But I can't accept that harmony. It's not worth the tears of the children, because those tears are unatoned for. They must be atoned for, or there can be no harmony. . . . From love of humanity, I don't want that harmony. . . . Too high a price is being asked for harmony; it's beyond our means to pay so much to enter on it. And so I hasten to give back my entrance ticket. . . . It's not God that I don't accept, Alyosha, only I most respectfully return Him the ticket. . . .

"Tell me yourself, I challenge you—answer. Imagine that you are creating a pattern of human destiny with the object of making men happy in the end, giving them peace and rest at last, but that it was essential and inevitable to torture to death only one tiny creature . . . and to found that edifice on its unavenged tears. Would you consent to be the architect on those conditions?"

"The longing for belief" was to be resolved by the conversion which began for Dostoevsky with his experience in the Katorga. There for the first time he looked into the real depths of human nature and saw all its frightfulness. It was in this context that he perceived the cardinal meaning of the problem of morality. His "merciless examinations of his own self" showed him the hidden contradictions and dangers within the average human soul, the conflict between reason and instinct, and the regenerative force of suffering. He came to believe that man is an irrational element in Creation, and that his nature and destiny are determined by powers which cannot be comprehended by reason, let alone guided by it.

He realized the Promethean pride and the fatal illusion of atheism: that in freeing man from belief in God it delivered him over to superstitious faith in the man-idol. Unable to bear the forlornness of being orphaned and abandoned, Dostoevsky looked for something to replace atheism, something that would restore to life purpose and meaning. He found it in faith.

In the process by which the "Karamazov rebellion" was purified into belief in God, Dostoevsky depicted his own spiritual purification. Like Dostoevsky in prison, Mitya Karamazov suffers for a crime he has not actually committed. And as Dostoevsky came to the true path out of his sufferings in Siberia, Mitya too discovers in prison the new man within himself, which "would never have come to the surface if it hadn't been for this blow from heaven."

Mitya's anxious talk with Alyosha, when he tries to clarify his attitude towards the premises of his atheistic friend Rakitin, reproduces Dostoevsky's state of mind in Siberia. "A new era is beginning," Mitya says. "That I understand. But still I am sorry to lose God. What will become of men then, without God and without immortal life? All things are lawful then, they can do what they like. . . . But the thought of God is tormenting me; that's the only thing that's worrying me. What if He doesn't exist? What if He's an idea made up by man? Then man is the chief of the earth, of the universe. Magnificent! Only how is he going to be good without God? That's the question. I always come back to that. For whom is man going to love, then? To whom will he be thankful? To whom will he sing the hymn? . . . What is goodness? I only wonder how people can live and think nothing about it?"

Out of questions such as these sprang Dostoevsky's entire religious credo: that man cannot live without belief in God. Without God, without the assumption of a planning spirit wisely governing Creation, the whole universe, he felt, would be a conglomerate set in motion by blind natural forces, and human life would be a product of chance, meaningless and purposeless. And if there were no higher meaning, there would also be no higher attachments for the guidance of moral and spiritual life; all standards, all morality, all possibility of discrimination between good and evil, would vanish. No longer responsible to a higher ethical authority, man would be motivated purely by transitory worldly interests; he would do whatever he pleased. Then in actual fact all things would be lawful; every crime would be permissible, and all values would be devaluated. To strive for perfection, truth, and goodness would be quite beside the point; for to give meaning to life presupposes a higher idea, the idea of God, and all values are sustained only by it and in it. All nobility, all culture, receives its strength from the idea of God and strives to reach that idea.

"Not a single nation has ever been founded on principles of science or reason," Dostoevsky wrote in *The Possessed*. "Science and reason have from the beginning of time played a secondary and subordinate part in the life of nations. Nations are built up and moved by another force which sways and dominates them, the origin of which is unknown and inexplicable. It is the force of the persistent assertion of one's own existence. . . . It is the seeking for God."

The same humanitarianism which once sent Dostoevsky into the camp of the atheists later led him to recognize that by revolting against God in the name of human happiness and seeking to replace divine ideas by human ideas, humanism violated the true destiny of man. His undeviating love for humanity ultimately led him to belief in God; only by religious faith could he retain his belief in an inalienable meaning, in the dignity and truth of man. For only in love for God was the true love of neighbor and of all humanity possible. Only by the creed that we are children of God do we all become brothers. "The secret of the brotherhood of all is contained in the common Father, in God."

Dostoevsky did not keep his religious thinking cooped up within the confines of theological theory. With his genius for recasting all experience into art, he also transformed the experiences of the mind into characters and events. He pointed out the intellectual bankruptcy of atheism by dramatizing its actual tragic results. Out of the degeneration of morality to a nihilistic "All things are lawful," out of the desolate orphaned state of the godless man, he made the drama of murder, suicide, and insanity—an intellectual drama of Shakespearian proportions played against the awesome set of a dead universe.

The monologue of *Notes from Underground* is a kind of prelude to this tragedy of disbelief. The cellar door opens, and the underground man steps forth into the upper world as Raskolnikov. The intellectual monologue is transposed in *Crime and Punishment* into dramatic action. The underground man appears disguised as a poverty-stricken student; he employs the logic of enlightened rationalism, and cloaks his criminal desires for power under the high-sounding phrases of idealistic humanism.

"I am not one of those who abandon the weak to the scoundrels. I come to the aid of the defenseless. . . . I cannot coldbloodedly pass by all the horror, all the suffering and wretchedness of people, and not say a word," Raskolnikov exclaims. He feels himself destined for great deeds, which he needs power and money to accomplish. He decides to kill a despicable old pawnbroker "who only does harm to people," and to rob her of her money. "Of all the insects in the world I have chosen the vilest, and in killing her I intend only to take as much as I need for my first step to power." Since he proposes to use the money for the benefit of innocent sufferers, he thinks himself justified in committing murder and theft. "Would not one tiny crime be wiped out by thousands of good deeds. . . . One death, and a hundred lives in exchange—it's simple arithmetic!" These words which Raskolnikov overhears in a tavern express his own trend of thought.

"I have not killed the old woman, but the principle," he cries autocratically. But after the deed, the cloak of noble motives is dropped. Raskolnikov's murder was merely the practical application, the experiment, designed to prove the hypothesis which the underground man had worked out in his cellar. But it is also meant to show that the man who decides questions of good and evil by his own judgment and who permits himself everything, ultimately loses his usurped freedom, and by destroying another destroys the humanity within himself.

In *The Possessed* Raskolnikov's Siberian nightmare is converted into social actuality. The godless arbitrariness which stops at nothing is here made the doctrine of a new social order; the nihilistic voice of the underground man swells to a chorus; the license which granted Raskolnikov the right to individual crime in the name of human happiness is here extended to collective crime committed for the sake of the future welfare of the masses. We are given the social analogy to Raskolnikov's personal tragedy. Within the broader framework of social events the same blasphemy is committed. The curse upon men who have lost God turns their vaunted freedom into mass enslavement and leads to mutual destruction and mass exterminations.

Stepan Trofimovitch Verhovensky—the decayed representative of a faith that has lost its vitality—begets the monster Peter Verhovensky for son, that false Moses who was handed his new tables of the law—"All things are lawful"—in the dark cellar of the underground man, Shigalov. He shows the new humanity a promised land flowing, not with milk and honey, but with human blood.

"When the gods fall, the demons emerge." In the traits of various types, in the intellectual leaders, fellow travelers, executives, and victims of a society that has lost God, Dostoevsky portrays the destructive rule of the unleashed demons.

Peter Verhovensky destines Stavrogin for the ruler and idol of this godless society. Stavrogin is, so to speak, naturally endowed with the characteristics of an apostate from God. Stavrogin is one of those who are, as the Apocalypse has it, neither cold nor hot, and must therefore be spewed out. Soulless, without any stirrings of emotion, he has the hollowness and detachment of a wooden idol. No rebel against God, but godless from indifference, impotent even in his doubt, "he believes when he doubts and doubts when he believes." He lacks all scruples and any ability to make moral distinctions. Without passion, without even the illusory justification of any ideals, he agrees to Verhovensky's doctrine of general destruction for the attainment of lofty ultimate goals. He himself is capable of the vile crime of driving to suicide an innocent, maltreated little girl whom he has raped. He lets her go into a room, looks at his watch, waits twenty minutes, and then peers through a crack and sees what he had to see, that the little girl has hanged herself. "Sitting at tea and chatting with the crew, for the first time in my life I clearly formulated the following for myself: I have neither the feeling nor the knowledge of good and evil, and not only have I lost the sense of good and evil, but good and evil really do not exist for me."

Since he was incapable of repentance, Stavrogin could not receive the grace of redemption by purification. His personality breaks down into shadowy emptiness, his heart is numbed, his days—filled by nothing—become a vacuum, "a boredom verging on the unbearable." To escape it he hangs himself, removes himself "from the earth like a horrid insect."

As a complement to Stavrogin in *The Possessed*, Dostoevsky created the character of the fanatical martyr to atheism, Kirillov.

In Stavrogin's history Dostoevsky indicated that loss of belief in God necessarily led to loss of a feeling for life. In the character of Kirillov he carries the inexorable logic of atheism one step further. For Kirillov is not satisfied with mere doubt. The simple theoretical denial of a higher will seems to him insufficient guarantee of the ultimate liberation of humanity from the yoke of God. Kirillov will not accept vague promises of the future benefits of man's rule instead of God's. He wants practical proof that God does not exist; he thirsts for radical action, for man to take power at once.

If there is no almighty God, Kirillov argues, God's omnipotence must necessarily accrue to men. "If God does not exist, then I myself am God," he concludes. ". . . The attribute of my godhead is self-will. . . . If God exists, all is His will; if not, it's all *my* will, and I am bound to show self-will . . . the summit of my self-will."

But Kirillov, who will show himself and the world that he is independent of any supreme power, has to resort to voluntary death. His "sacrificial death," a suicide influenced by no outward circumstances and committed out of pure self-will, is to be an example for all mankind, the grand demonstration of man's sovereignty when he is freed from fear of God and terror of death. "I am killing myself to begin; I will reveal my self-will and will open the door."

The sole proof that this Promethean atheist can offer for his autonomous self-assertion is suicide; for him, existence free from

God is the freedom of nonexistence. A corpse inherits the place of the deposed divine ruler of the infinite universe. The message for humanity in his "sacrifice" is the message of the anti-Christ. In contrast to the "joyful tidings" brought by the true Redeemer, the God-man, the tidings of the resurrection of the soul to eternal life in God, this man-god redeemer sends a gloomy pledge of the self-annihilation of man and his dissolution in nothingness.

The nullification of the idea of God leads to man's self-destruction. That is the lesson of *The Possessed.* Dostoevsky shows another aspect of this self-destruction in *The Brothers Karamazov.*

In Ivan Karamazov it is reason itself that suffers the penalty of the negation of God. Ivan's brilliant dialectical intellect disintegrates, and he turns into a schizophrenic. But this psychic phenomenon is not described by a psychoanalyst; it is transformed by an artist into dramatic event. Ivan's negation of God is projected outward and assumes concrete form: the first denier of God, the devil, appears to him in the flesh, and advances all the philosophical arguments for Promethean atheism, for the "all things are lawful," for the insubstantiality and nonexistence of everything that cannot be grasped by human reason.

During the conversation with the devil, Ivan notices with growing disquiet that every argument the devil presents is actually Ivan's own, his own philosophy. As an amusing illustration of the denial of God at any price, the devil tells an anecdote. Ivan recognizes that this anecdote was once made up by himself. "I've caught you," Ivan cries out in a fury. "You want to make me believe that you exist. But you don't have any independent existence. You are my hallucination and nothing else. It's I myself speaking, not you. You are the incarnation of myself, but only of one side of me . . . of my thoughts and feelings, but only the nastiest and stupidest of them. You're I, I myself, but with another face."

On the one hand Ivan's denial of God leads to the breakdown of his intellect, to madness; on the other hand it results in intellectual responsibility for the murder of his father. For Ivan's godless theories influenced Smerdyakov to commit his crime.

When Ivan is horrified at Smerdyakov's confession, Smerdyakov replies: "You yourself always told me that everything is lawful. Why are you so surprised now?" Smerdyakov accused Ivan: "You murdered him; you are the real murderer. I was only your tool, your faithful servant."

Just as the devil was the incarnation of Ivan's atheistic intellect, so the crime of this moral Caliban, Smerdyakov, was the materialization of his atheistic principles.

The turn of Dostoevsky's mind was such that it could entertain both Ivan's atheistic arguments and Mitya's horror of a world without God. In Christ he found a solution to the tormenting alternation between belief and disbelief. Just as for Augustine and Pascal before him, there would have been no way out of his spiritual dilemma but for Christ, who alone had made it clear "what God is and what man is." Christ was the mediator through whom Dostoevsky attained to faith in God. It was during the Siberian interlude that he read a great deal in the New Testament, and was deeply moved by the figure of Christ that emerged from it.

From prison he wrote to Madame Fonvisina, telling of his doubts and of his consuming longing to believe. He referred also to "those moments of grace" when the thought of Christ brought him a perfect calm. "At such moments," he wrote, "I enfold in my heart a symbol of faith which makes everything bright and holy for me. This symbol is very simple; it consists in believing that there is nothing more beautiful, more profound, more lovable, more reasonable, more courageous and perfect than Christ." And in his first revulsion against atheistic rationalism with its pretentious claim to omniscience, he closed his letter with the words: "More than that; if anyone proved to me that Christ was not in the truth, and it really was a fact that the truth was not in Christ, I should rather be with Christ than with the truth."

For to Dostoevsky Christ was a proof of God which outweighed all the arguments of speculative reason for or against his existence. In Christ the transcendence of God became earthly reality; the divine became other than the concept of the Ideal, a mere figment of the intellect or a creation of logic. In Christ the divinely timeless became a temporal event—the figure, life, and destiny of a man. This absolute faith in the God-man, which Dostoevsky first formulated in the *Meditations on Christ,* later became the principal affirmative idea of all his works.

"I am the way, the truth, and the life!" These words of Christ, which Sonya read aloud to Raskolnikov, accomplished his conversion and rebirth.

"Christ," Shatov retorts to the atheists, "came only so that humanity would learn that nature too, the human mind, can actually appear in divine splendor and not only as ideal, and that all this is natural and quite possible. Those who followed after Christ were able to endure the cruelest torments and still bear witness to what a blessing it is to aspire toward the perfection of Christ and to believe in His existence in the flesh. That is what it is all about—that the Word was made flesh in reality. In that is the whole of faith and the whole consolation of mankind, which men can never do without." And at the close of *The Possessed* Luke's parable—of the men whom the shepherds found at Jesus's feet, after their demons had been exorcised and driven into the swine—is a pledge of society's recovery through faith in Christ.

The great aim Dostoevsky set for himself in his fiction was the presentation of Christ in modern guise. He wanted to create a character of perfect evangelical purity inhabiting this present world of chaos, a wholly human person who had, however, the aura of a higher existence. He attempted such a Christ-figure in Prince Mýshkin. A more mature trial was Alyosha, whose plain, meaningful life of faith and love is intended as a rebuttal to Ivan's dialectic. Dostoevsky was revealing another aspect of Christ in the *Legend of the Grand Inquisitor*, which he himself called the "culmination" of his work as an artist.

The principles of atheism are incisively analyzed in the dialogue between Ivan and the devil. But analysis alone is not enough for Dostoevsky; he takes the spirit of negation and embodies it in an actual physical devil. He does something similar in *The Grand Inquisitor* where the principle of divine truth is embodied in the real presence of Christ returned to earth. In a marvelous scene the grand inquisitor, who has reversed the Redeemer's doctrine of love in behalf of man's earthly happiness, goes over all the points where he is at variance with Christ, and gives his justifications for a secularized Christianity. During this long monologue his adversary Christ remains silent, says not a word in reply to all the grand inquisitor's reproofs—and triumphs in the end by His very silence. For Christ has no need of words or arguments to prove His truth. "He Himself is the truth."

For Dostoevsky Christ was "so beyond all cavil" that he could not imagine even an atheist's being able to dispense with Him. Neither the sentimental atheist Hippolyte in *The Idiot* nor the cynic Stavrogin in *The Possessed* could reject Christ. And the fanatic atheist Kirillov declares: "Listen: that Man (Christ) was the loftiest of all on earth. He was that which gave meaning to life. The whole planet, with everything on it, is mere madness without that Man. There has never been any like Him before or since, never. . . ." It is the ingrained agnostic Ivan who writes *The Legend of the Grand Inquisitor*. And even the devil, who embodies Ivan's atheism, keeps himself from paying tribute to Christ "solely from a sense of duty and my social position." "I was there," the devil says, "when the Word Who died on the Cross rose up into Heaven bearing on His bosom the soul of the penitent thief. I heard the glad shrieks of the cherubim singing and shouting hosannah, and the thunderous rapture of the seraphim which shook heaven and all creation, and I swear to you by all that's sacred, I longed to join the choir and shout hosannah with them all. The word had almost escaped me, had almost broken from my lips . . . but common sense—oh, a most unhappy trait in my character—kept me in due bounds, and I let the moment pass! For what would have happened, I reflected, what would have happened after my hosannah?"

Worship of Christ was also the keystone of Dostoevsky's political creed. "If we do not acknowledge Christ we shall err in everything," he wrote. "The way to the salvation of mankind leads through His teachings alone. There have been and are many leaders of humanity, but the great and final ideal of human development, of the development of the whole human race, is to bring about what He taught and lived."

There is a story pertaining to the end of Dostoevsky's life, when he had been acknowledged as the nation's spiritual leader. He is supposed to have attended a ball at a secondary school in Petersburg. As soon as he entered, the story goes, the dancing came to a stop, and the music, too, faltered and was broken off. The young couples came to him and asked him to talk about Christ. And so he spoke of "Christ's truth" in the ballroom until dawn.

At apparently the same time that Dostoevsky wrestled with, and conquered, rationalistic doubt in the Katorga, another great doubter in the far north issued from a similar struggle with "a decisive victory of faith." Kierkegaard's report is also contained in a letter: "My whole being is transfigured. . . . I must speak. . . . I know now that I have found God in Christ, and that He will help me to triumph over my doubts."

Although they never heard of one another, Kierkegaard and Dostoevsky used almost the same words to express their revulsion against the arrogance of rationalism, and to confess their faith in a truth that speculative logic could never grasp—the proof of God through Christ. The faith in which all of Dostoevsky's works is steeped was also the core of Kierkegaard's existential philosophy. Both men must be counted among those great preachers of a religious rebirth to whom we in this troubled age turn with hope.

PART II

DOSTOEVSKY'S SIGNIFICANCE FOR OUR TIMES

CHAPTER FIVE

DOSTOEVSKY'S PLACE IN MODERN FICTION

D OSTOEVSKY'S time fell within the era of the birth of the modern novel. Stendhal, who pioneered the new form, had been dead only two years when Dostoevsky published his first novel, *Poor Folk*. This came hard on the heels of Gogol's *Dead Souls*. Gogol went insane and died at about the time that Dostoevsky's first period came to an end, for the writer was then ready for the ordeal in Siberia. Coevally with *Poor Folk* there appeared the first volume of Balzac's *Comédie humaine*, and this same Balzac reached the highest point of his creative life, in his *Cousin Pons* and *Cousine Bette*, when Dostoevsky was writing *The Double*.

At one and the same time Dostoevsky, Dickens, Flaubert, Zola, Hawthorne, Tolstoy, and Turgenev were at work. Dostoevsky was writing *The House of the Dead*, Flaubert *Salammbo*, Turgenev *Fathers and Sons*, and Dickens *Great Expectations*. *Crime and Punishment* bears the same date of publication as Tolstoy's *War and Peace* and Zola's *Thérèse Raquin*. Shortly before, Hawthorne had published *The Marble Faun*, whose theme was akin to the problem of *Crime and Punishment*. And at the moment that Dostoevsky was sketching the plan for his cycle of novels, *The Life of a Great Sinner*, Zola began *Les Rougon-Macquart*. Dostoevsky's *The Idiot* appeared in the same year as Flaubert's *l'Education sentimentale*; the publication of *A Raw*

61

Youth coincides with that of Flaubert's *Tentations de St. Antoine* and Tolstoy's *Anna Karenina*. And during the time Dostoevsky was laboring over his last and artistically most important work, *The Brothers Karamazov*, Tolstoy was writing his *Confessions* in which he virtually renounced the profession of writing.

The novel in the modern sense, which made its triumphal entry into literature in the nineteenth century, aimed at dispensing with idealistic heroes who performed before romantic stage sets. Instead it tried to describe faithfully the true human being in the environment of everyday life with all its realistic aspects and social miseries. Each of the great conquistadors of modern literature carved out a new province of reality.

No sooner had Stendhal (that "perceptive genius with his sure grasp of facts who was so much ahead of his time," as Nietzsche called him) incorporated into the novel the world of *petits faits vrais*, than he was followed by the creative colossus Balzac. In his cosmos, populated by almost two thousand characters, Balzac drew up a complete inventory of all human instincts and passions. He assembled "the greatest archive of documents on human nature that we possess."

Zola, in his *Rougon-Macquart* cycle with its more than twelve hundred characters, expanded the boundaries of Balzac's *exactitude documentaire*. His naturalism took up for the first time the brutal undercurrents of life by which men are propelled. He mapped the milieu of rising industrialism. Flaubert enlarged the domain of art to include the poignance of profane life. Gogol, the founder of Russian realism, exposed life's shabby aspects. Tolstoy described the sensual world of physical man, Turgenev the cruel indifference of universal nature to petty human suffering. Dickens photographed the actual through the filter of human temperament. Hawthorne studied the effect of realities upon the moral nature of man.

Along with this change in the subject matter of the novel, the nature of the artist's problems and his very approach and sensibility changed. Glorification of life was replaced by stress on its negative aspects—evil and baseness. Instead of abstractions, the crudely sensual came to the fore. Highly contrived plotting was abandoned in favor of plotless development following the natural course of events. Exaggerated emotionality went out and sober objectivity came in. Literary language was superseded by the tone of common speech. Some writers tried to achieve the new effect of trueness to life by exhaustive study of each smallest detail; others by precise reporting and an analytic procedure based on the practice of the exact sciences; still others by adopting the manner of the chronicler, putting down both important things and trivialities with the same reliability.

For Stendhal the ultimate truth about man is his rationally guided ambition; the basic motive underlying all his actions is egoistic fulfillment of his self-love. Stendhal's hero in *Le Rouge et le Noir*, Julien Sorel, is motivated exclusively by the desire to rise out of his environment and win power and mastery over the world. (Julien reappears, wearing the clothes of the Louis Philippe era, as Lucien Leuwen, and we meet him once more in the character of Fabricio del Dongo in the *Chartreuse de Parme*.) Love, intelligence, strength of will, goodness, as well as criminality, are solely means to the attainment of this one goal in his life: success.

From his stupendous cast of characters Balzac extracts the basic laws of human nature. His people are all slaves of grand passions concerned with the surest means for obtaining their desires—money. The pursuit of money is the most powerful of all passions. For money is the center of the Balzacian cosmos toward which all his *hommes de passion* strive, no matter how different they may otherwise be; their common and fundamental trait is their *préoccupation de l'argent*. The ambitious Rastignac in *Le Père Goriot* is determined mercilessly to override any obstacle on the road to the power that money can buy, and Lucien de Rubempré in *Les illusions perdues* is ready to sacrifice his soul's salvation for the happiness that money assures.

Stendhal, then, objectively and with an amoral impartiality takes note of man's ruthless nature; Balzac raises the factor of ruthlessness to gigantic proportions. He displays a certain admiration for its elemental force. The moralists among the realistic writers, each according to his temperament, describe the same phenomenon either with indignation or mockery, with pessimistic fatalism or with pious hope of improvement.

Zola, the social moralist, drew in *Les Rougon-Macquart* the group portrait, through several generations, of a family consumed by ambition and greed; he decided that baseness is the primal clay out of which the demiurge Nature fashioned men. He thought that his picture of "the beast in man" conveyed the only faithful likeness of the individual. And he visualized the habitat assigned to that individual, the industrialized metropolis, as a modern jungle inhabited by human beasts of prey. Zola's diligent collection of facts and the scientific exactness of his descriptions served again and again to prove "the supremacy of the digestive and reproductive mechanisms over the mind."

Gogol, ancestor of the morality-centered Russian realism, saw the repulsive face of life. He drew fierce caricatures of man the beast. Ambition was for Stendhal an extension of intelligence; Balzac saw it as the outgrowth of intense passions; Zola apparently classed it among the natural instincts. But for Gogol ambition was only the grotesque expression of "immortal human insipidity." Miserable scoundrels, petty rascals, job-hunters, careerists, and liars are the inhabitants of a Dantesque inferno of daily life; a shabby devil is the chief executive of this hell. That is the real world of Gogol.

To Tolstoy, the "great seer of the flesh," the reality of life is contained in biological nature. Tolstoy has a unique eye for external appearance, which for him beautifully expressed all psychological processes. Physical traits correspond to traits of soul and mind. A delicate, attractive figure symbolizes the esthetic sensitivity of his female characters; the well-rounded head, the strong back and shoulders, stand for the more complete, rounded-off male character; the puffed-out chest betrays inward hollowness; hasty movements indicate mental restiveness; a lax body in a woman represents a soul lost in the duties of daily life. In the physical sufferings of Ivan Ilyitch, which Tolstoy documents with the crudest realism and the accuracy of a pathologist, all the sadness of the human creature is shown.

In sensual pleasure in living and in animal fear of death, in horror at the dissolution of the body and in the fertility by which life wins out against death, Tolstoy sees the whole mystery of earthly existence.

In the flesh and in the world of property which is arranged to serve fleshly life, the later Tolstoy, the sensualist turned moralist, saw the fundamentals of the ethical problem. He concluded that desires and lusts were the chains of Satan, and that they would have to be forcibly broken to bring about the liberation and salvation of the individual.

In Flaubert's novels reality is composed of the banal events of daily life. His protagonists are Madame Bovary, the little provincial who becomes an adulteress out of dissatisfaction with the monotony of her life, and who pays by suicide for her transgression against bourgeois morality; or the empty, wholly insignificant youth in *l'Education sentimentale* who becomes aware, after years of unconsummated love, of the happiness he has missed. In order to reproduce faithfully the unimaginative existence of the average, Flaubert renounced any life of his own. To set down every tiniest trait and every most trivial nuance in the hearts of his characters, Flaubert employed a language incomparably musical, and a style that may be termed the greatest in the literature of the world.

His Russian counterpart, Turgenev, applied his subtle talent for the analysis of mood and his remarkable aptitude for word-painting to rueful, realistic appreciation of the frightfulness and lack of meaning of ordinary life.

An island segment of life—the teeming world of Victorian London—formed Dickens's model for his realistic pictures of big cities. The suffering of the poor, relieved by noble-hearted men of good will; the intrigues of evildoers, over which the virtue of the good and upright ultimately triumphs; society's abuses, knowledge of which is tempered by a comforting faith in progress which will bring everyone middling happiness—the drama of life translated into melodrama is the realistic subject matter that Dickens mastered in his works. This "greatest genius of the heart" wrote with such human sympathy, such a vigorous grasp of character, and such sunny humor, that he was able to reconcile his readers to life.

Reality "seen through the Puritan temperament," which subjected every action to the stern analysis of conscience and saw behind the sinful act a deeper inner moral problem—this was the subject of Hawthorne's realistic novels.

Dostoevsky's novels share the realistic background which was the common property of his age. "Little" people are his heroes: the unromantic world of daily life is their sphere. The fierce struggle of self-will with society, the poverty and misery of early nineteenth-century capitalism, and the base nature of man in all its various forms, elemental evil as well as drab rascality and the wretched little weaknesses of men, supply him with the stuff of life for his novels.

In their ambitious striving toward personal happiness Raskolnikov in *Crime and Punishment* and Arkady Dolgoruki in *A Raw Youth* are blood brothers of Stendhal's Julien Sorel, Balzac's Lucien Rubempré, and Zola's dreary careerists in *Les Rougon-Macquart*.

As it was for Julien Sorel, for Raskolnikov, too, power is synonymous with happiness. Their dreams follow the same lines —they want to achieve on a small scale what Napoleon achieved on a large: getting power at the expense of others. Julien Sorel's exclamation even in the shadow of the scaffold, "There is no law outside of the natural law of man," is a declaration of faith hardly different from Raskolnikov's when he knows he has been condemned to Siberia but has not yet experienced purification.

For Dostoevsky's ambitious heroes money is the shortcut to power, the best guarantee for the gratification of all passions and lusts, as it is for Balzac's and Zola's heroes. Like Rastignac, Raskolnikov is convinced that "a man's moral code depends on his purse," and that it is necessary to have money to stand above all moral laws. The raw youth Arkady Dolgoruki also wants "to break through the wall," to trample across all moral prejudices. For "what harm can there be in it if the millions fall from a dirty and ruthless hand into the firm and sensible hand of another who knows how to enjoy his power?"

Balzac's cynical embezzler Vautrin asks Rastignac the famous question whether he would have resolution enough to murder an unknown mandarin, in order to get the money he wants. This question corresponds exactly to the considerations Raskolnikov turns over in his mind before he decides to kill the "unknown mandarin"—the old woman pawnbroker—in order to lay hands on the money he wants.

Like Balzac's and Zola's heroes, the lovers of Natasha Fillipova think they can buy love by money, and Dostoevsky's great *homme de passion*, Dmitri Karamazov, has even resolved to kill his own father for the sake of the money with which he hopes to buy Grushenka's favor.

But the very similarity of social types and of motive and destiny throws into sharp relief the basic dissimilarity of Dostoevsky's characters. True, he interests himself in similar social situations, but his realism is realism with a difference. It is this difference that underlies the unique manner in which he treats the problems of ambition, power, and money. Above all, there is the uniqueness of his personal concern with the fate of his protagonists.

Stendhal, Balzac, and Zola trace the obvious course of lives governed by ambition and the passions; Dostoevsky describes the spiritual events that are focused in the specific fates of his ambitious and passionate heroes. For the others, the problem of self-will is a socio-psychological problem flowing from a particular social situation. For Dostoevsky it is a metaphysical problem, and the basic dilemma of human existence is inherent in it. The French realists describe the conflict between the community and the unbridled individual; Dostoevsky is concerned with the moral defection of the egotistic will from divine Being and from the commandment imposed upon the whole. The others' analytic procedure reveals the psychological mechanism of ambition and passion; Dostoevsky brings to light the primal elements of human nature, out of which ambition and the passions are compounded.

In the novels of the French realists the truth about human nature is translated into a sociologic, psychologic, or anthropologic idiom; Dostoevsky's novels offer the original text.

The portrayal of crime and its consequences, which has always been the "grand subject" of world literature, thus became the main theme of the realistic novel, which was in any case devoted to the "night sides" of human nature. Stendhal's cold intellect viewed crime as the logical consequence of a life governed by self-will. Prison and the guillotine appeared to him as the revenge of society upon the rebelling individual.

To Balzac crime was the dynamic discharge of titanic forces. With visible pleasure he fits out his criminals with social honors and dignities, titles of nobility and high positions.

Zola, "the scientific criminologist," threw light upon the natural history of the criminal act. In *Thérèse Raquin*, in which the heroine must atone for murdering her husband with the help of her lover, he describes even the torments of conscience as a brutal external process. In his murderer, Jacques Lantière, Zola deliberately created a figure to contrast with Raskolnikov. He wanted to prove that the instinct to kill is, along with the erotic drive, the motivating force of human nature.

Dickens, who condemned evil with all the abhorrence of a well-conducted citizen of old England, portrays his criminals as unequivocal representatives of Evil, whose wickedness is branded even on their outward persons. Their sole emotion is selfishness and vengefulness. And just as his good characters are amply rewarded, his wicked ones are punished. When Dickens died the Bishop of Winchester could say that his novels might be given to any child, because they served effectively to warn against crime.

Dostoevsky's first great novel, *Crime and Punishment*, deals with a murder; his last novel concerned the most terrible of all crimes, parricide. And most of the principal figures in his other works are either actual criminals or potential ones, criminals in wish and thought. Dostoevsky, who knew the power of evil from having lived with convicts in Siberia, knew more about crime than did any of his contemporary realists. It was clear to him that "crime is not a mere social disease, but is moored deeper in human nature than the social physicians of optimistic humanism are willing to admit; the inclination toward evil for evil's sake is an ancient, fundamental force in man's being."

Dostoevsky believed that will and the criminal act were only self-evident variations of a fundamental metaphysical principle. He took man to be "the arena where Satan—the principle of fundamental evil—and God—the principle of fundamental good —strive for mastery, and the battleground is the heart of man." Thus the source of crime was transferred from outside to inside man. In the works of the other realists, society sits in judgment; in Dostoevsky it is the penitent conscience. The problem of crime and punishment is transformed in Dostoevsky's works into the problem of guilt and atonement.

Stendhal's criminals are rational, determinate types, un-checked egoists. Balzac's characters are "Linnéan species of crime." Zola's criminals are at the mercy of the killer instinct. Dickens's scoundrels are marionettes of Evil. What happens to these characters is the outcome of their pre-established nature. Dostoevsky's metaphysical conception of the primal struggle between the evil and good principles in man brings to light the more complex dual nature of the individual in conflict with himself. The personal history of his criminals is the dramatic working out of this conflict. Dostoevsky's realism took the criminal type and made a real character out of him.

In Stendhal, Balzac, Zola, and Dickens the criminal goes to his doom, commits his crime, and receives his punishment. After these writers have followed their characters through all the ups and downs of their lives, subjected them during each phase of their development to the subtlest psychological analysis, and noted the smallest incident in their careers, they stop short after the de-scription of their tragic destruction. For them the novel is over. But it is here, where the others' concern for their characters leaves off, that Dostoevsky's real interest in his criminals is aroused. At that point he reveals his deep psychological insight, and his amazing ability to convey character. The external action which led to the crime and its punishment is to him merely the prelude to the real action, which starts within the hero's conscience after the deed. The outward collapse, which forms the dramatic close in the works of the others, Dostoevsky utilizes for the accomplishment of his heroes' moral and spiritual destiny. Dostoevsky's attack on his problems begins where the others stop.

Repentance and the moral awakening which succeeds crime was also one of Hawthorne's main problems. In fact, Hawthorne is more akin to Dostoevsky than any of the other novelists who were his contemporaries. Hawthorne's *The Marble Faun* and Dostoevsky's *Crime and Punishment* are strongly alike, both in theme and in the course of action. Donatello, the protagonist of *The Marble Faun*, like Raskolnikov becomes aware of the dark recesses of his nature only after the deed is committed. Both figures find their true personality in the purgatory of repentance.

But Hawthorne's handsome, careless, immaculate youth Donatello, "a faunlike being," incurs his guilt only by an almost accidental murder. For Raskolnikov the intellectual source of his crime is the germ of guilt. In Raskolnikov's amoral ambition, in his hatred for the "contemptible, ugly old woman," the axe lay hidden. It was there all the time, waiting for the trembling hand of the criminal student to raise it for the death blow. The crime was consummated in his mind before the act itself; the actual murder was merely the pragmatic result of his criminal thoughts.

Hawthorne's primary interest was the reality of man's moral nature. *The Marble Faun* studies the evolution of an untroubled creature who, through sin, wins his way to the possession of soul and conscience.

For Dostoevsky, moral reality was but one aspect of the metaphysical reality which is present even before it condenses into the actual moral drama. Raskolnikov, who is debased through guilt and reborn through understanding, is the prototype of man, who separates himself from God and returns to Him in repentance.

"By some incomprehensible witchcraft I am cut off from life," the author of *The Marble Faun* confesses in a letter to Longfellow. This lonely, introspective man, who had no experience with life's actual lower depths, meditated upon crime, punishment, and atonement rather in the manner of a "habitually thoughtful" Puritan. The theme as carried out in *The Marble Faun* adds up to the moral doctrine of a Puritan rebel; the work turned into a religio-moral parable, with symbolic characters who "flowered in the secluded shade of a withdrawn life."

Dostoevsky felt the murderous passions within his own heart; he had within himself the living experience of Raskolnikov's crime, was his murderer's accomplice in spirit. It is no accident that three earlier versions of *Crime and Punishment* were cast in the first person; the final third-person form was a later refinement. Through his complicity, Dostoevsky was able to describe Raskolnikov's atonement and purification with the compelling force of a personal experience. So credible was his description that a Moscow intellectual who had robbed a bank and been sent to prison justified himself by referring to Raskolnikov's arguments. Another—a student who had committed a crime—found his way to repentance and atonement after reading *Crime and Punishment*.

The salient factor that sets Dostoevsky's work apart from that of his contemporaries (though, as we have shown, certain situations and characters obsessed them all) was the metaphysical conception underlying the Russian's novels.

"Le roman est une durée qui se défait." Thibaudet's comment on the French novel is relevant, with few exceptions, to the realistic novel in general. The novel describes a span of life which passes meaninglessly and is self-defeating. But in Dostoevsky's novels events that seem meaningless suggest ultimate meaning; they imply that there is something eternal behind the ephemeral things we see, that a spiritual law governs all chance.

For the other realists truth lay in keenly observing what there was to see. For Dostoevsky this is not so. His way of looking is best described in Blake's words: "I query my physical eye no more than I would query a window when I am looking out of it. I look through it and do not remain in it."

Dostoevsky's literary contemporaries lacked his personal familiarity with social wretchedness as much as they lacked his knowledge of crime. Dostoevsky, that boarder in the house of hunger, and blood-brother to the insulted and injured, fully knew all the horrors of poverty. But his stark depictions of poverty did not come to a dead end in explanations of its socio-economical significance. He treated the moral tragedy in the light of the primal spiritual tragedy of human nature. And economic misery too was for him a fragment of the whole spiritual tragedy of man. What he cared about was how the human mind responded when its plea for daily bread went unheard—that plea which is the only petition for material goods in the whole of the Lord's Prayer. And he does not see avarice merely as an outgrowth of social corruption; it is metaphysical pollution, the bondage of the living spirit in lifeless matter.

Stendhal had already recognized the power of the intellect— in fact was the first to do so—and had made a study of it in his novels. But he was a rationalist, and could handle only its secular, rational aspect. Dostoevsky applied himself to its metaphysical content. The ideas that dominate Raskolnikov, Myshkin, Stavrogin, Kirillov, Shatov, Versilov, and the Karamazovs are not abstractions of their personal traits, but archetypes of the passions. The motives of Stendhal's heroes are of the world; Dostoevsky fetches his ideas from the realm of the Faustian "Mothers."

Although the desires of Dostoevsky's *hommes de passion* may also be directed toward some definite happiness, in reality his men are always the victims of *la passion de l'infini*. Their wish for earthly goods occupies as negligible a place as it does in the Lord's Prayer. They are almost entirely occupied with their longing to be forgiven their trespasses, to be delivered from evil.

Dostoevsky's characters, whether saints or murderers, wise men or idiots, are deeply religious persons. The central problem of their lives is God, whether they affirm or deny Him. Their closeness or remoteness from God determines their place in life, more than their social or economic situation or the level of their culture. The conflict which results from their relationship to God also constitutes the essential conflict of their daily life. Metaphysical indecision is the agony resulting from their inner duality; the crucial decision of their lives is the solution of the problem of God.

And yet, though Dostoevsky's picture of life and people is essentially a picture of ideas in conflict, those ideas never remain intellectual categories; their validity is never a matter of theory; the problem of faith is never stated as a theological doctrine, nor as an ethical principle. The ideas are always presented in the form of dynamic passions; each intellectual battle explodes into powerful drama. The things of the spirit become existential event and concrete gesture.

In their *passion de l'infini*, which is inherent in all their secular passions, Dostoevsky's characters, like himself, know no moderation. Always and in everything "they overstep all boundaries"—the line between the attainable and the ideal, between the empirical and the transcendental, between the rational and the irrational, between reality and dream or delirium. In their lives the commonplace easily slips over into the fantastic, the normal into the extreme, and fantasy and hallucination quickly become integral parts of their real existence.

Expanding the factual world of the other realists to include the vast world of subjective factors, adding events of transcendental origin to the simple cause-and-effect phenomena, introducing the element of the fantastic, Dostoevsky enlarged the domain of reality.

"Certainly reality is more important than anything else, but it may be that I have a wholly different conception of reality and realism than all our realists," he wrote when critics charged his novel *The Idiot* with "fantasticality." "What most people call fantastic and eccentric is for me often the true essence of reality. And perhaps in *The Idiot* of all my works I have succeeded in showing man in a way most true to life, more real than what is commonly called reality."

While the dogmatic realists were pushing back the boundaries of the world of the novel to take in new provinces of reality, Dostoevsky's "imaginative realism" was giving the novel a new dimension, the dimension of inner reality. And as he saw people and life in a light that was all his own, his technique of representation was also all his own.

The other writers in their "transcript of the factual world" used outward traits as the starting point for describing their characters. They gave the reader the results of their keen observation. Their heroes are like masterful portraits; the details are all beautifully delineated. Thus the Duchess Sanseverina in Stendhal's *Chartreuse de Parme* reminds one of "a painting by Correggio." Tolstoy was justly called the "Rubens of the Russian novel." There are scarcely any situations in Tolstoy's novels in which he omits sensuous description of his people. And in the Homeric tradition, he uses the recurrent epithet to help us visualize his characters.

Henry James writes of Turgenev's manner of description: "An idea with him is such and such an individual, with such and such a nose and chin, such and such a hat and waistcoat, bearing the same relation to it as the look of a printed word does to its meaning."

Pickwick's embonpoint and his gold waistcoat buttons are as much a part of his personality as the sash around Kutusov's waist in *War and Peace*. Tolstoy considers it appropriate to mention the stains a baby has left on its diapers, and Dickens faithfully notes the spot on the waistcoat.

In giving a detailed description of the clothes of two fops, Balzac drew up a definitive report on the latest fashion. In describing the broad, flat surface of Charles Bovary's coat, Flaubert conveyed all the flatness of his personality. This novelist devoted several pages solely to the description of a nightcap. Frequently, in Balzac, Dickens, and Gogol—literary portrait painters who worked mostly from models—repressed romanticism led them into fantasy or caricature. But even then their exaggerations stayed inside the framework of realistic conditions. It was a case of raising visualized reality to the level of fantasy. They exaggerated as artists exaggerate—like Michelangelo, who gave his huge figures more muscles than they have in nature, in order to intensify the impression of strength; or like Goya and

Daumier, who used satirical distortion to convey an emphatic external resemblance.

Ambitious to outdo all the other realists, Zola the naturalist went beyond their technique of portraiture. "I shall paint a picture of the physiological man, who is nothing but an aggregate of histological elements," he proclaimed. Zola added the sense of smell to the equipment of the realist. Here was a new faculty to help take in the phenomenal world. Zola took as his model the physician Claude Bernard, "who searched voluptuously for each individual nerve fiber of the stinking, living flesh." The novelist analyzed and described the specific effluvia of the human body: the odor of sweat of a woman's back and armpits, the aroma of the foods his characters ate, the smells of their offices and factories, which clung to their clothes, and even the odor of sexual intercourse. He believed that such exactness in art was the way to get at the real nature of people.

When Dostoevsky created character, he started with the psyche, the emotions and thoughts of his figures. Often he did not bother to describe what they looked like; he sketched in their appearance briefly and roughly. Occasionally he did use a physical trait to mark character, such as "the double chin and the drooping flesh bags under the small, always suspicious and spiteful eyes" of old Karamazov, the sensualist. But this sort of description was tossed off casually compared to the detailed care with which the personality itself is described. Even where Dostoevsky took live models for his characters, he copied the psyche rather than the physical being.

In order to achieve a total picture, his contemporaries chronicled every daily activity of their figures. The reader sees them awakening in the morning. In Paris he attends the levee of the parvenus. In Russia he is present when Ivan Nikoforovitch "puts on his trousers, has his cravat tied, and finally squeezes into his jacket; as he does so the seam under the arm splits." The reader goes with them to the bedchamber at night and has an opportunity to observe them in the act of love, as through the peephole in some Parisian brothels. In their private rooms they are never out of our sight for a moment. And we are also privileged to witness all their activities outside the home. We stroll or hasten down the street with them to their government bureaus, business offices, or factories; we see them toiling or idling at their work; we see them in their leisure time, eating, drinking, or amusing themselves; and we know all about their economic conditions.

The Russian authors offer accountings like faithful stewards of the movable and fixed property on their heroes' country estates. Like a bookkeeper, Balzac balances debit and credit, the profits and losses of his entrepreneurs' business speculations; like a usurer he calculates the interest on their loans. He exposes the household budget, tells us how much the tailor bills and the rent come to, how much is paid out to each tradesman, so that we know exactly how much each character spends for his living. These writers, to dramatize the poverty of the poor, turn out their pockets, and the few sous or kopeks that fall out are carefully counted.

About Dostoevsky's characters we have no such intimate knowledge. We don't know when or how they sleep or whether they sleep at all; we don't know what they eat and drink, or how they behave in sexual intercourse. What we are told about their occupation and social position is often little more than a passport would show. Profession: student, army officer, priest, merchant. They are rich, moderately prosperous, or destitute; but Dostoevsky gives us no extracts from property records, no bank statements, no debt register, or other documents to prove how wealthy or how poor they are. Never is there a hint of how much they spend for a living.

Dostoevsky ignores all these *petits faits vrais* because he does not equate the real nature of people with their physical characteristics and their activities. He sees their nature as emerging from what they say, from the Word, that physical element which borders on the metaphysical. The words people say reveal the invisible reality of their psycho-spiritual make-up. Dostoevsky forms his characters after an image that he has captured through hearing, by perceptive listening. The way he establishes his characters as concrete and true to life is by the amazing faithfulness of his picture of the psyche.

We see them vividly in terms of the inner tensions which they discharge in explosive, angry dialogues, or resolve by forgiveness and understanding; in terms of their doubts and shifts in a dialectical game of pros and cons; and in terms of the certainty of their faith, which becomes their "hosanna." Spoken thoughts materialize into fateful acts; intimate confessions are made; opinions clash violently—such are the "events" that keep the action of the story moving forward. Like terminal rhymes, words conclude a development, words cast lots and determine destinies.

The "real life" characters in the novels of Dostoevsky's contemporaries strike us as familiar because they correspond to our memory of actual people, or because we have experienced in ourselves their psychic life, their duality, their sins of thought, their doubts. In the complex of problems Dostoevsky's heroes must master we confront the problems of our own mind. "All the things we are forbidden by caution, self-respect, and atavistic inhibitions suddenly leap up at us out of Dostoevsky's books, as out of the darkness, and seize us with savage, indescribable power," Powys writes trenchantly. "Everything we have felt but not dared to think; everything we have thought but not dared to say; all the frightful whisperings of the unmentionable borderline areas, all the terror of the unexplored depths, rise up and overwhelm us."

This realism of Dostoevsky's, the poetic reconstruction of his characters' inner world, so overwhelms us that we forget to ask about the omitted physical descriptions. Nor does it occur to us to wonder about the missing information on time, place, and scene.

Unquestionably the description of the Russian tavern in *The Brothers Karamazov* is sparse and casual, compared to the vividness of a similar description in Gogol, in which tables, chairs, and every single patron is carefully pictured. But in the Karamazov tavern we are so under the spell of Ivan's conversation with Alyosha about belief and doubt, ultimate good and ultimate evil, that we would rather shut our eyes to listen better to the dialogue. For what the two brothers discuss at the tavern table abruptly recalls and clarifies the unsolved problems that have always haunted humanity. As they speak we seem to see all the hosts of heaven and hell gathering to contend over man's fate; this dialogue in the tavern anticipates the decision that is not to be made until the Day of Judgment. Is this still a definite Russian tavern at all, where particular people at such and such a time carry on such and such a conversation with one another, or is it the extra-spatial room within our own soul, where the timeless human spirit talks to himself about his eternal problem?

Virginia Woolf's English temperament was at first repelled by Dostoevsky's "formless, confused, diffuse and tumultuous" manner; but she came to recognize the incredible alien power of the Russian. She writes: "The novels of Dostoevsky are seething whirlpools, gyrating sandstorms, waterspouts which hiss and boil and suck us in. They are composed purely and wholly of the stuff of the soul. Against our wills we are drawn in, whirled round, blinded, suffocated, and at the same time filled with giddy rapture. . . .

"As we read we pick it all up—the names of the people, their relationship—but what unimportant matters these are compared with the soul! It is the soul that matters, its passion, its tumult, its astonishing medley of beauty and vileness. The elements of the soul are seen not separately but streaked, involved, inextricably confused; a new panorama of the human mind is revealed. . . . Out it tumbles upon us, hot, scalding, mixed, marvellous, terrible, oppressive—the human soul."

Dostoevsky's method of making the climaxes of his novels erupt within the extravagant intellectual processes of his characters requires a new kind of plot, different from the usual epic development of the realistic novel. Even so impetuous a genius as Balzac conformed to the logic of step-by-step narration; but in Dostoevsky's novels the action usually takes place as a succession of explosive outbursts. Proust remarked that Dostoevsky never presents things in logical, causal succession like other story-tellers; instead of beginning with the cause, he often shows the effect at the outset.

We make the acquaintance of most of Dostoevsky's characters when they are violently agitated, when they have had disastrous collisions with the world or with each other, when their feelings have reached the point of excess and driven them toward crime or madness, when they are reacting to extreme situations and are heading toward frightful ordeals.

Dostoevsky's technique of character analysis is radically different from that of Stendhal, who selects a few samples out of the untidy aggregate of emotions and offers them tidily separated and laid out for us to examine. Dostoevsky touches off the chained powers of the elements and demonstrates their explosive dynamism.

In the world of his novels time is not measured by the clock, but by the changes of inward states. The striking of the passions marks morning, noon, and night in the soul. Not the past in epic narrative, but the present shown with dramatic immediacy, is the content of his novels.

"Un roman est un miroir qui se promène sur une grande route," was Stendhal's definition of the genre. Accordingly, he made the action in *Le Rouge et le Noir* extend over several years. In Dostoevsky's *Crime and Punishment* the action is compressed into one week; the tragedy of *The Brothers Karamazov* takes but a few days; and all events in *The Idiot* happen between morning and midnight.

Dostoevsky disapproves of epical spans of time; he gives each event an extraordinary temporal density. In novels based on people's external lives, problems will take years to develop and be resolved; in Dostoevsky's novels the whole process of development and resolution is often concentrated into a few hours. Sometimes the duration of a single dialogue contains the abundance of a whole life.

He sets aside the tranquil, even course of narration; instead there is a breathless rush of action. The few breathing spells the reader is allowed resemble the intermissions between the acts of a play.

At first glance Dostoevsky's work seems lacking in architectural balance. If, however, we take an undogmatic view of the construction of his novels, another but no less strict structural

principle is seen—that of tragedy. His method of beginning with
the effect rather than the cause is the root principle of classical
drama; the action which follows in a series of abrupt discharges
serves the same purpose as the technique of suspense used by the
great tragic dramatists, who give their characters freest rein before
pulling them sharply in, back to the center, to the inescapable
dénouement.

The sparseness of his descriptions appears to be in accordance with Aristotle's advice—that even the epic poet has need of
dramatic discipline and compression, so that "the loosely-con-
nected form will achieve artistic unity." Dostoevsky conforms to
the rules of tragedy, not only where he slights the canon of the
epic, but where he goes beyond it. His descriptions of place are
sometimes as curt as the placards exhibited on the Shakespearian
stage. His description of the appearance and clothing of his characters is usually no more than a brief stage direction. On the
other hand, the brooding, tortuous soliloquies of his heroes recall
Hamlet, and the monologues and choruses in Aeschylus, So-
phocles, and Euripides. As in the great tragedies, everything in
Dostoevsky's novels turns on the troubles of the heart, and the
outward fate comes as the fulfillment of the inner destiny. When
the Moscow Theater staged several scenes from *The Brothers
Karamazov* it was able to use the actual text of the novel without
change for the stage production.

Dostoevsky's work is a milestone in the history of the novel.
His dramatic "interior" concept of reality rounded out the nineteenth century's realistic art, and at the same time opened new
roads for the modern novel; it foreshadowed the psychological,
expressionistic, surrealistic, and fantasio-realistic techniques.

The writers who were drawn to him and those he repelled,
as well as those who appear to bypass him, are equally in his debt.
Even among the greatest and most individual writers there are
few whose fictional world fails to show the traces of Dostoevsky.

The Russian *Double* walks abroad again in Stevenson's
Dr. Jekyll and Mr. Hyde and in Julien Green's *Voyageur sur la
Terre*. Raskolnikov, absolved, marched away with Sonya to forge
his soul's salvation in Siberia, but in England and in France his

ghost would not be laid. In Stevenson's Markheim he once more murders a pawnbroker, recognizes his guilt, and experiences a moral regeneration. As Greslou in Paul Bourget's *The Disciple* he commits another murder under the sway of an abstract idea. We find him again in Joseph Conrad's *Lord Jim*, the handsome Englishman who vainly struggles to break with his own inner foe, and in Hugh Walpole's *Prelude to Adventure.*

We hear the voice of the underground man in Gide's *The Immoralist*; Michael, the hero of this novel, leads us to the edge of the chasm of the psyche, and we catch sight of the strange beasts that inhabit it. Infected by Ivan Karamazov, Monsieur le Perrone in Gide's *Counterfeiters* rebels against the indifference of a God who permits so much cruelty and suffering in life and hides his true purpose. And Passavant and Edouard in *The Counterfeiters* display the same traits as Stavrogin and Ver-hovensky.

The damned soul of Stavrogin passes through its literary karma. It is incarnated in the figure of George in D. H. Lawrence's *White Peacock*, in the character of Brinn in Beverley Nichol's *Crazy Pavement*, and in Spandrel in Huxley's *Point Counterpoint*, whom the author himself describes as "quite a little Stavrogin."

Neil Adam in Somerset Maugham's *Ah, King* so obviously strives to imitate Alyosha that Daria tells him to his face, "You are a little Alyosha yourself."

There are French derivatives of the Russian tribe of the insulted and injured. Charles Louis Philippe pleads for the class with some of Dostoevsky's passionate pity, and the little prostitute in Philippe's *Bubu de Montparnasse* is a French cousin of Sonya Marmeladov, still another in the line of "noble-hearted whores."

D'Annunzio, who held the theory that anyone not of Latin blood was a barbarian, could not entirely escape the influence of the "barbarian" Dostoevsky, who in his turn had pronounced the Russian Asiatics first in all things of the spirit. And at the northern outpost of Europe, Strindberg fell thoroughly under Dostoevsky's spell. Strindberg courageously followed the Russian down into *The Inferno* of the soul.

Jakob Wassermann's heroes are made of the same soul stuff as Dostoevsky's, and the dualistic Dostoevskian solution to their problems make Wassermann's great novels "exciting dreams." In Malraux's *Conquerors* we see the transposition of psychic adventure into revolutionary action, as in *The Possessed*.

Virginia Woolf takes as scene for her novels that invisible realm that Dostoevsky revealed; the experiences of mind and soul comprise the action, and the time sequence of the psyche replaces clock and calendar. It was Dostoevsky who built the psychic chute down which Joyce's streams of consciousness and the unconscious flow. Dostoevsky's interior monologues educated our ears to hear the Joycean soliloquies.

The metarealistic elements that Dostoevsky recognized are transformed in Kafka's fragmentary novels into the "Law," the "Castle," the "Court," those symbolic forces of destiny his orphaned heroes try vainly to approach.

Dostoevsky's own peculiar realism drew in the outline of that order "in which life and death, the real and the imaginary, the high and the low are no longer felt as contradictions"—the order proclaimed by Saint Paul-Roux's ideorealism and by Breton's *Surrealist Manifesto*.

In Russia symbolists like Bryasov, Sologub, and Andreyev betray the influence of Dostoevsky, and Alexander Blok in his powerful visionary poem, *The Twelve*, identifies the Russian people with Christ just as Shatov does in *The Possessed*.

Jean-Paul Sartre, exponent of French existentialism, stated: "Dostoevsky wrote: 'If God does not exist, then all things are lawful.' That is the starting point of existentialism. For with the disappearance of God there also disappeared all possibility of finding values in an intelligible heaven. This world of abandoned man who cannot find anything to hold on to, neither within himself nor outside of himself, is the world of the existentialist novel."

CHAPTER SIX

DOSTOEVSKY—A FORERUNNER OF PSYCHOANALYSIS

DOSTOEVSKY has been accused of a "cruel talent." He has been blamed for taking sadistic pleasure in dwelling on the sinister, chaotic, and morbid regions of the psyche. There alone, it is alleged, he feels himself really at home. No less than forty different abnormal characters have been counted in his works. "It is open to question whether literature has the right to concentrate on morbid, exceptional cases," de Vogüe wrote; and a number of critics followed his lead, ridiculing Dostoevsky for his portrayal of "the world as a kind of insane asylum."

Recent progress in the science of psychiatry has given us a deeper understanding of the anomalies of the psyche. Psycho-analytic expressions have become part of everyday speech. Libido, trauma, aggressive instinct, compulsion, ambivalence, repression, complex, introversion, fixation, regression, and overcompensation—by becoming conventional terms these words have taken away some of the uncanniness of the mind's confusions and contradictions. With psychic factors given their due even in our daily life, we see Dostoevsky's "cruel talent" in another light. We recognize it as the first realistic insight into heretofore unknown areas of the soul. And we cannot help seeing that Dostoevsky anticipated many of the discoveries which psychoanalysis, psychiatry, and character analysis have only recently made after prolonged clinical observation, investigation, research and psychological tests.

Certainly the man who did this pioneering started from a set of postulates entirely different from those of the positivistic psychologists and psychiatrists. All psychic phenomena were for him manifestations of superior metaphysical realities. In portraying abnormal states of the psyche he was not interested in describing sicknesses *per se,* nor in recording the minutiae of "psychological case histories." His intention was rather—as it was also in his studies of crime—to reveal a primal tragedy of the mind and soul. For Dostoevsky mental disturbance suggested not the medical problem of how to save the patient's mind, but the religio-ethical problem of saving an afflicted soul. His knowledge was obtained not from objective observation but from his own experience and suffering. The ills of the disturbed psyche which psychiatry defines and classifies under names such as erotomania, manic depression, grand and petit mal, dementia senilis, allopraxia, infantilism, hysteria, megalomania, pseudologia phantastica—these were seen by Dostoevsky in terms of tragic characters: Murin, Raskolnikov, Rogoshin, Stavrogin, Stepan Trofimovitch, Natasha Filippovna, Lisa Hohlakov, Lisa Drosdov, Kirillov, Ivolgin, Marmeladov, and Smerdyakov.

It was in the eighteen-sixties that modern psychiatry was initiated by the famous Professor Charcot, whose sensational Tuesday soirées at the Paris Salpetrière dealt with the newly discovered phenomenon of the "abnormal psyche." In Charcot's time the science of abnormal psychology was still umbilically linked to physiology. Yet in distant Russia the writer Dostoevsky was already several steps ahead of the learned professor. In his *The Double, The Landlady,* and *Notes from Underground* Dostoevsky had already grasped the irrational nature of psychic phenomena. He had shown how motivations operated dynamically, in obedience to distinct laws of their own.

Sigmund Freud, who was to develop Charcot's discoveries into the modern science of depth-psychology, was born in 1856. He was still a boy going to the *gymnasium* when Dostoevsky's novels *Crime and Punishment, The Idiot,* and *The Eternal Husband,* with all their wealth of psychoanalytic illustrative material, had already been written. When Freud received his medical degree from the University of Vienna in 1881—the year of Dostoevsky's death—Dostoevsky's complete works already contained a mass of material which was later to loom large in Freud's doctrines.

Analytic science has more or less codified the psychic common law of the Dostoevskian world. In this world people hate those they love and love those they hate; they kill those whom they are ready to die for, and take the tenderest care of those they want to kill. Obeying hidden and contradictory impulses, they do what they are trying to avoid; and avert, for reasons they themselves do not understand, what their conscious will is striving for. They are aware of the utter senselessness of an action even while they are trying with all their might to carry it through. Out of their declared intentions there springs up like a jack-in-the-box the latent, true intention. They betray themselves by apparently meaningless "blunders," "absent-mindedness," "slips of the tongue," and "forgetting." Almost always the events in Dostoevsky's novels read like blueprints for the later doctrines of psychoanalytic textbooks.

In this world of Dostoevsky's, little girls cry out with unconscious childish eroticism, "Do whatever you want with me, tyrannize over me, pinch me just once, my little sweetheart." Adolescents with unsatisfied desires try to "abreact" their torment by torturing the beloved, and then punish themselves for this outlet by jamming their fingers in a door. Their fits of laughter end, in accordance with the laws of hysteria, in sobs; their libidinous drives, repressed into the unconscious by conventional morality, take covert paths in the attempt to outwit the watchdog of consciousness. Harried by obsessions, these people must commit compulsive actions; after a murder, for example, they return repeatedly to the scene of the crime. Occasionally they sublimate their base impulses in acts of nobility; occasionally the dammed-up current of their pleasure principle changes direction, and forces a way out in the guise of the death instinct. Their vices are intermingled with their virtues, their wisdom with their folly. In their confessions they make use of the same type of "free association" that Freud evoked from his patients. In *The Eternal*

Husband, in a chapter significantly entitled "Analysis" Velchani-
nov the lover examines with Freudian penetration the motives of
the cuckolded husband, Pavel Pavlovitch, who has come to visit
him. "He wanted to kill me, but didn't know he wanted to kill me.
It's senseless, but that's the truth. Yes, it was from hatred that
he loved me; that's the strongest of all loves. . . ." The Freudian
"primal deed," King Oedipus's murder of his father, is also the
dynastic primal event in the "bourgeois" ruling family of the
Karamazovs. All phases of the primitive drive to parricide are
demonstrated in the three sons, and studied down to the subtlest
volitional stirrings and thought associations. "Everyone has the
desire to murder his father," Lisa Hohlakov remarks in this
novel.

Freud's *The Interpretation of Dreams* appeared at the turn
of the century, in 1900. Thirty-six years earlier, when Dostoevsky
made Raskolnikov conceive the murder of the old woman pawnbroker, he showed his character dreaming a "regressive dream"
of childhood that perfectly fits Freud's ideas. In the dream
Raskolnikov is walking past a tavern with his father. He sees
drunken peasants whipping a horse to death, and clutches his
father's hand anxiously. When he wakes he recognizes the warn-
ing of the dream, and exclaims in horror at his murder plan, "I
couldn't do it." Free for a moment from the compulsion of his
fixed idea, he prays, "Lord, show me my path. I renounce that
accursed dream of mine."

"The interpretation of dreams is in reality the *via regia,* the
royal road to knowledge of the psyche," Freud wrote. Dostoevsky
had already set out upon this road in *Crime and Punishment.* "In
a morbid condition of the brain dreams often have a singular
actuality, vividness, and extraordinary semblance of reality," he
writes as preface to this first dream of Raskolnikov.

After the act of murder Raskolnikov deflates his bold
Napoleonic claims in a "reduction dream." He re-experiences his
crime in a dream that mockingly devalues the act. In the dream,
as he strikes the old woman, she begins to shake with "uncanny
noiseless laughter," and goes on laughing as he hits her again and
again. In the dream his mind was already accepting what his

waking intellect still refused to admit: the madness and deceptiveness of his theories of the exceptional man's "right" to commit crimes.

Even before the decisive transformation has taken place in Raskolnikov's waking consciousness, the dream mind has already announced the inner change in its abstruse figurative language. In the Siberian prison hospital Raskolnikov has the horrible dream in which his own depravity becomes a plague infecting the whole world. This dream comes to him on the eve of his regeneration.

The psychoanalytic dream mechanism is shown in full operation in the dream that the voluptuary Svidrigailov has just before his suicide, when he is thinking about violating a child. For contrast, the dream has birds chirruping under the hotel window, while on a table in the middle of the room stands the coffin of a dishonored girl who drowned herself because she was unable to bear her shame. In the hotel corridor Svidrigailov comes upon a child who is cowering in a corner, weeping. He pities the little girl, takes her and puts her to bed in his room. Then he notices that the child has the unchildlike face of a French harlot. She opens her eyes and turns a shameless glance upon him; she holds out her arms and laughingly invites him. "What, at five years old!" he cries, raising his hand to strike her—and wakes.

Stavrogin, Svidrigailov's kinsman in vice, who rapes a twelve-year-old girl and coldbloodedly lets his victim commit suicide, makes a confession to Father Tihon in a scene reminiscent of a psychoanalytic session. For a long time his crime left him completely indifferent. He did not think about it until one day when he was traveling in Germany he "absent-mindedly" forgot to change trains and so traveled on a railroad line that was not along his "planned route." He got off at a strange station, went to an unfamiliar hotel, and fell asleep. He had a strange dream. A painting by Claude Lorraine that he had seen in a Dresden gallery was transformed in his dream into an actual scene. The painting had represented happy, innocent people in a paradisiacal landscape. Then the scene shifted from the idyll to the figure of a tiny red spider on a geranium leaf. And suddenly his victim stood before him, haggard, with feverish eyes, shaking her head reproachfully and lifting her tiny fist in a threatening gesture. He remained under the spell of the dream all night. "Call it conscience or call it repentance—I don't know," he confesses. "Since then I see the vision almost every day. . . . It will continue like this until I go mad."

In *The Idiot* the dream of Hippolyte, the psychopathic consumptive whom the doctor has given only a few weeks to live, reveals behind the "manifest content" of the "dream façade" the Freudian "latent content." A seven-inch-long reptile creeps from the wall of his bedroom toward Hippolyte. He flees; it follows and pursues him until it touches his hair. He calls for help. His dog, dead for five years, comes running up and snaps at the reptile. The dog gets bitten in the tongue, but succeeds in biting the creature in two. The two parts continue to writhe in the dog's mouth.

Prince Myshkin, the hero of *The Idiot,* makes observations in 1870 about the nature and function of dreams. His remarks sound like those a modern intellectual familiar with psychoanalysis might make. "Why is it that when we awaken and return to reality, we almost always have the strong feeling that back of the dream something inexplicable remains?" he asks. "We laugh at the absurdity of our dreams and at the same time we feel that there is an idea interwoven with these absurdities, a real idea, something that belongs to actual life, something that is and always will be in the heart. It is as if something new that we've always been waiting for has been said to us in the dream."

Arkady in *A Raw Youth,* that walking textbook example of the father complex, fixation, libido, repression, and ambivalence, is well aware that his dreams afford the best insight into his real condition, and that their figurative language pronounces an irreversible verdict of his unconscious mind. Ostensibly he is striving after the ethical life; in a dream the "horrid spider" is revealed which is secretly spinning its web within him. "This dream," Arkady decides in a sort of self-analysis, "proves that in my heart all these things were already germinating; they were there in my desires, but in the waking state my heart was still ashamed of them and did not dare to realize anything of the sort consciously. In the dream, however, my soul revealed what was in my heart and showed it in the vivid images of truth."

In *The Brothers Karamazov* Alyosha is deeply disturbed at the sight of his saintly teacher's decaying corpse. The shock to his senses is sublimated in a dream to spiritual and religious ideas. As he kneels at the bier of Elder Zossima, listening to the passage from the Gospel about the marriage at Cana, his tormented and contradictory emotions are transformed into a dream vision of the joyful wedding feast in which the dead Elder takes part and invites Alyosha to join the rejoicing. Alyosha leaves the bier a man transformed by his dream.

In *The Dream of a Ridiculous Man* the would-be suicide has a "compensatory dream" in which his morbid despair is transformed into a life-affirming religious attitude. Anticipating the psychoanalytic interpretation of dreams, the dreamer realizes that "not the intellect but the wish guides the dream and makes use of strange tricks to achieve its aims; overleaping time, space, and all the rules of reason, it dwells only on those points that our heart dreams of."

"Dostoevsky's views on the dream and his dream analysis have not been surpassed to this day, and his idea that no one thinks and acts without a goal and without an ultimate climax, is in accord with the modern findings of psychology," writes Alfred Adler. For Dostoevsky even anticipated Adler's individual psychology, which is a further step in the development of psychoanalysis and dream interpretation. Adler perceived that the "eternal woes" of mankind cannot be "cured from this one point [sex] alone, that the will to self-assertion, the ego libido's drive for power, plays certainly no lesser and probably a greater part in the psyche than the Freudian sex libido." Dostoevsky had presented this hypothesis half a century earlier in the behavior of many of his characters. Foma Opishin in *Stepanchikovo Village*, Raskolnikov in *Crime and Punishment*, and Arkady in *A Raw Youth* manifest all the typical signs of social sensivity, the lust for power, inferiority complexes, and overcompensation. "Everyone who sees how Dostoevsky completely grasped the tendency to despotism which is inborn in the human psyche," Adler declares, "must acknowledge him as our teacher to this day."

Freud made us aware of the power of the sex libido over the unconscious regions of the psyche. Adler did the same for the Caesarean power of the ego libido. Carl Jung with his "complex psychology" tried to go even farther, down to the realm of the Faustian "Mothers." He pointed to the spiritual creative force that had set up the sex libido, the ego libido, and whatever other psychic structure might yet be discovered. Beneath the chasms of the individual psyche Jung discovered, as the primal base, the incomprehensible and yet pragmatic motivating force which was superindividual: the psychic energy of the collective unconscious; religious conceptions and the power of imagination. Jung's contribution was to add an important new dimension to the realm of scientific psychology—dimensions that Dostoevsky had already charted in his fiction.

"The psychic alone qualifies as immediate reality. This holds for every form of the psychic, even 'unreal' conceptions and ideas. Calling such contents imaginary or delusory takes away no whit of their effectiveness; in fact, there are no 'real' thoughts that in some cases may not be thrust aside by 'unreal' thoughts, proving that the latter have greater energy and effectiveness than the former. Worse than 'perils of the soul' are the colossal effects of delusory ideas, even though our consciousness or 'reality' denies these ideas all reality. The powers-that-be which rule all humanity for weal or woe are unconscious psychic factors, and it is such factors that bring forth our consciousness and thereby the *conditio sine qua non* for the existence of any world at all. . . . The imagination, which is both emotion and thought, therefore seems to me the most distinct expression of specific activity." These sentences of Jung's might easily be excerpts from Dostoevsky's works, his letters to Maikov, or his *Diary of a Writer*.

The "inner voice in which the natural and the false is intermingled," and which, according to Jung in his *Integration of the Personality*, "plunges the soul into deepest abysses of confusion, deception, and despair," is the voice of the director in Dostoevsky's novelized tragedies. Jungian "introversion" is the crucial problem of many Dostoevsky characters. It is the "cellar," the underground place from which sounds the voice of a sulking soul, a soul that has withdrawn itself. "Raving reason" leads Raskolnikov to crime, Verhovensky and Shigalov to mass crime, Kirillov to suicide. Almost all of Dostoevsky's characters are the protagonists and victims of their unreal thoughts and ideas, slaves of their dreams, prisoners of their *idées fixes*. In Maria Lebyadkin, the mad girl whom Stavrogin has married, introversion reaches the pitch of actual insanity. The confrontation of the intricate, inward, imaginative life with "true living life" was the basic idea of Dostoevsky's planned *Life of a Great Sinner*. In *A Raw Youth* this treatment was applied to the character of Versilov.

In his treatise *The Unconscious in the Normal and the Sick Psyche* Jung finds that, "The loss of belief in God releases dangerous forces which previously were bound and fastened to the divine image and now take the road into the unconscious. Mass murder is then what this unconscious charged with psychic energy makes of it." In *The Possessed* Dostoevsky showed precisely that: the dangerous outlets of men who rebel against God.

Psychiatrists have marveled at Dostoevsky's exhaustive descriptions of epilepsy, which date from a time when science knew almost nothing about the psychology of the epileptic. "Among writers there has probably never been any who understood the sick psyche so well, who was a greater psychologist than Dostoevsky," said the medical journal *Berliner klinische Wochenschrift*. This estimate has been confirmed by analysts of the caliber of Freud, Adler, Steckel, and Rank, all of whom have praised Dostoevsky's astonishing penetration into the nature of the unconscious.

CHAPTER SEVEN

DOSTOEVSKY'S PROPHECIES

IN THE present crisis of humanism Dostoevsky's works are as pertinent to us as anything written by our contemporaries. His novels talk about things we are experiencing and suffering from today. We have seen Dostoevsky's underground man arise to shatter the humanistic heritage of our civilization; his "possessed" are in our midst. The problems of his Russian fictional world have become universal problems of today's real world. In the intellectual and emotional crises of his heroes whole classes and nations see their present plight dramatized. Danger and anxiety pervade his novels; danger and anxiety are basic to our age. And the downfall of civilization which he grimly foretold has come, in our time, to seem an ever-present peril.

During the past few decades our inner and outer security has been repeatedly shaken; and our respect for Dostoevsky's writings has grown with each shock. Each successive disaster brings us to a deeper understanding of him; both in tone and content he seems like one of us, one of our more desperate contemporaries. There is no disparity between his problems and our own. If we turn to his books more and more nowadays, it is not as students of literature; we search them for present-day values and meanings. Men at odds with themselves and their times look to Dostoevsky's novels for instructions concerning the precarious future of our civilization. Christopher Hollis was wholly in earnest when he said at a session of the British Parliament: "Every prospective M.P. should be required to pass an examination in Dostoevsky before being elected."

The title of "prophet," first conferred upon Dostoevsky by the enthusiastic crowd who heard his Pushkin address, has stayed linked with his name, and events after his death have borne out his right to it. Many of the greatest Russian thinkers, however they might differ in their allegiances, saw Russian history as fulfilling certain of Dostoevsky's prophecies. This tendency persisted even into the era of bolshevism. In the Soviet memorial published for the hundredth anniversary of Dostoevsky's birth we find: "Today we read *The Possessed,* which has become reality, living it and suffering with it; we create the novel afresh in union with the author. We see a dream realized, and we marvel at the visionary clairvoyance of the dreamer who cast the spell of Revolution on Russia. . . ." And Lunacharsky, first Russian Commissar of Culture, wrote at the time: "Russia goes forward on her thorny but glorious way, and behind her stand her great prophets. Among them, the most enthralling and splendid of all, rises the figure of Fyodor Dostoevsky."

The age of religion looked upon prophecy as a gift of God; the romantic era saw it as clairvoyance, the gift of second sight; to the rationalistic epoch it was a subtle psychological phenomenon, the product of unconscious reactions of the brain, evoked usually by morbid conditions which so intensify perception that the smallest signs in the present are recognized as portents of future events. The psychiatrist Pierre Janet called it a *"fonction du réel."* In our scientific age it is interpreted—by Henri Bergson, Alexis Carrel, J. W. Dunne, Charles Richet, H. S. Saltmarsh, and others—as a factor which liberates the seer from the physical continuum and lets him "remember" within a four-dimensional space-time the future as well as the past. The latest word on the subject is the theory advanced by advocates of the modern guiding-field theory, who consider prophecy an interaction between the physical and immaterial guiding fields.

Whatever hypothesis we adopt, there is no doubt that since the days of the Old Testament every age has believed that certain chosen persons possess the gift of foreseeing events. Almost all great religious, spiritual, and political movements—the Messianic and millenarian movements of the past and the social movements of our time—have been influenced by prophetic annunciations. Individuals as well as the masses have been fired by prophetic suggestion with the unyielding faith and the burning will to make the impossible possible, to overthrow established social orders and replace them by new ones. The belief in progress arose out of Saint–Simon's and Comte's prophecies of a future positivistic paradise; liberalism and socialism grew out of the prophecies of the Utopian reformers. Though Marx might speak in terms of "dialectical laws," or "overproduction, falling rate of profit, fierce class struggle and the triumph of the proletariat"—back of these socio-economic concepts resound the eschatological predictions of world doom before the dawning millennium of a new earth.

Marx's collaborator, Engels, called *The Communist Manifesto* a prophetic document. No Marxist since has dared to question Marx's reputation as a seer. Faith in the fulfillment of Marx's prophecies brought communism into being. And the prophecies of Lenin, who claimed he could predict the day the communist paradise would be established, gave verve to the bolshevik revolution.

Those who are not under the spell of Marx the prophet, or who do not see the future as predicted in the *Manifesto* as altogether a paradise, can turn today to the writings of Dostoevsky. Dostoevsky was not only Marx's contemporary; he was, in the realm of prophecy, his antagonist. And it was Dostoevsky's forecast of our present-day world that was the more accurate.

How many of the prophecies in Dostoevsky's works constitute poetic truths, and how many of them have been confirmed by actual events and facts in our own time? When we look into this question, we must conclude that Dostoevsky was a genuine seer. Our respect for his predictions is increased when we consider the intellectual and spiritual situation out of which they arose.

A span of three generations separates us from the publication of Dostoevsky's first prophetic novel, *Notes from Under-*

ground, a span of two generations from *The Possessed* and *The Brothers Karamazov;* and in between appeared *A Raw Youth* and *The Diary of a Writer.* During that period there have been crucial intellectual, social, and economic upheavals, and out of the ferment has emerged our world, which is in many respects the direct antithesis of Dostoevsky's era.

The warnings contained in his work are today fulfilled prophecies; in his century those warnings could be shrugged off as the fancies of a confirmed pessimist.

The nineteenth century, whose main effort was directed toward economic happiness, saw "economic man" as representing the essence of human nature. His utilitarian aspirations were looked upon with favor, for were not these the surest guarantee of a harmonious future social order? The theoreticians of liberalism taught that man is by nature good and can act only for good; viewed in the proper light, his selfish interests coincide with the common welfare. Only let the machinery of the economy function freely, and the natural order of things would lead to constant improvement in the conditions of life, to the "greatest happiness for the greatest number."

In opposition to these hopeful views, Dostoevsky stated: "The time is approaching when the loftiest aims of humanity will be betrayed for temporal advantages. Humane feeling and striving for truth and justice will be surrendered, and a savage avidity for personal enrichment will take hold of men." And like one who has the terrible gift of foreseeing the death of those who are still strong and vigorous, he envisioned "the bankruptcy of the liberalistic dream of world happiness" in the very days of its most effective blossoming. The promised greatest happiness for the greatest number would, he foresaw, be converted into happiness for the privileged few at the expense of the many. He perceived that misery would result from the wealth of goods, that the new industrial productivity would create a new type of poverty. And where the liberals proclaimed a "harmony of interests," he saw taking shape two hostile camps. "These liberals do not suspect that soon an end will come to everything," he cried out, "to all their 'progress' and chatter."

Amid the capitalist security and tranquillity of his time he heard the rumbling in the depths. "The fourth estate is coming; it knocks and batters at the doors, and if they be not opened it will break the doors. . . . All this is 'near, at the gates.' . . ."

War in Europe seemed at that time remote. "Everybody predicts lasting peace," Dostoevsky wrote in 1876, "everywhere clear horizons, alliances, and new energies are being discerned. And yet Europe has never been so charged with hostile elements as in our time—as if the continent were undermined with dynamite and awaiting only the spark to ignite it. . . . In the long view lasting bourgeois peace inevitably evokes the urge to war. And not in the name of a great and righteous cause, but for the sake of certain trivial interests of the stock markets, for the sake of new markets that the exploiters wish to obtain, for the purpose of acquiring new slaves which the slave owners need in order to fill their money bags. . . . This unnatural situation will inevitably result in a huge political war in which all will be involved." And he went on to prophesy the coming World War which would be fought for imperialist aims, and its result—revolution: "Do you think society will be able to stand a long war? If the war drags on, millions of hungry proletarians will be thrown on the street. They will hurl themselves upon Europe, and all the old things will go forever. . . . There will be an overturn such as the world has not yet seen."

In *A Raw Youth* he sets down his prediction of the collapse of the capitalist bourgeoisie, an eventuality hard to imagine in the nineteenth century, but which later was to become a historic fact over half the world. "One fine day," Versilov says to Arcady, "in spite of all the balance sheets on budget day, and the absence of deficits, all the states without exception will be unable to pay, so they'll all be landed in general bankruptcy. At the same time all the conservative elements of the whole world will rise up in opposition to everything, because they will be the bondholders and creditors, and they won't want to allow the bankruptcy. Then, of course, there will follow a general liquidation; and then all those who have never had any shares in anything, and in fact have never had anything at all, will naturally insist on taking part in the liquidation. A struggle will begin, and after many battles the beggars will destroy the shareholders and carry off their shares and take their places as shareholders, of course. Perhaps they will say something new too, and perhaps they won't. . . . I can't undertake to predict the destinies by which the face of the world will be changed. Look in the Apocalypse, though."

In Dostoevsky's time all idealistic people who strove for a better social order put their hope in the new socialist movement. They considered that socialism would eliminate all the injustices of the liberal *laissez-faire* economy and introduce the millennium of liberty and justice.

Dostoevsky resisted this current of optimistic faith in socialism. He prophesied that the socialist movement would lead to an intensification of the crisis of humanity; to the complete loss of freedom that we are witnessing today in the totalitarian version of communism. What is most astonishing about Dostoevsky's prophecy is the fact that he knew the idea of socialism only in its purest and most idealistic form. He was familiar with Fourier's doctrine of association, the basic principle of which was, in the words of Considérant's *Manifesto of Peaceful Democracy,* "the dogma of fraternity." Dostoevsky also knew Proudhon's theory of a harmonious balance of interests; and he had read the federative socialists, who thought that the ideal social order of liberty, fraternity, and equality could be attained through scientifically devised organizations and institutions. In other words, Dostoevsky had read only the Utopian socialists.

The theories of these Utopian socialists, though widely different, had one thing in common: the belief that all existing social evils could be solved by a peaceful harmonization of contradictions, and that a new social order could be brought into being by an agreement to extend the rights of the workers, while preserving freedom for all classes.

True, in the February Revolution of 1848 the leaders of the French workers' party, Louis Blanc and Flaçon, departed from the doctrines of evolutionary reform socialism. But they clung to the idea that their revolutionary gesture was the "ruse of the mid-wife which would bring socialism's humanistic ideal of liberty for all more swiftly into the world."

The turning-point in the socialist movement came when Marx suddenly appeared amid the triumphal banners of the February Revolution. While the comrades were scattering humanitarian promises, Marx sneered at them, called them "alchemists of the Revolution," and dismissed their talk of harmonious development and their slogans of freedom for all as "sentimental humanitarian daydreams." Marx's concept of socialism was one of fierce class struggle which must end with the complete victory of the proletariat and total subjugation of all other classes. Instead of a peaceful fraternization of all classes, Marx called for a war-like alliance of the international proletariat; instead of a guarantee of freedom for all he wanted a dictatorship of the proletariat. He proclaimed that the downfall of the old world was the indispensable prerequisite for the rise of the new world order. Marx not only predicted this downfall; he himself was the beginning of the fulfillment of his prophecy. His doctrine of class struggle and dictatorship has shaped modern history.

Dostoevsky gave a prophetic description of the new direction that socialism was to take. Yet he had not read Marx and knew nothing of his theories. According to the testimony of the Marxists themselves, *The Communist Manifesto* of 1848 was not widely read until 1871. Its revolutionary significance was so little recognized, even among socialists in the West, that it was for long considered to be merely a paraphrase of Considérant's democratic manifesto.

The first Russian translation of volume one of Marx's *Capital,* which introduced Marx into Russia, was published in St. Petersburg in 1872, two years after the publication of Dostoevsky's novel on revolution, *The Possessed*. The story of the novel was suggested to Dostoevsky by the nihilist murder committed by Nechayev. Dostoevsky, however, wrote to his friend Maikov: "I must remark that the only sources of my knowledge of Nechayev or the circumstances of the murder have been the newspaper stories. But even if I had known the circumstances, it would never have occurred to me to copy them. My imagination is capable of extreme detachment from events as they take place in reality, and my Peter Verhovensky will not in the least resemble Nechayev."

Investigation of Russian conditions at the time has confirmed the fact that Russia in the seventies had no personalities corresponding to Verhovensky, Shigalov, and the others. The characters and the ideas they advocate in the novel must be considered purely imaginative adumbrations; only in our present time have they become reality.

Independently of Marx, and simultaneously with him, Dostoevsky arrived at a total condemnation of bourgeois capitalism. Like Marx, he predicted the inevitable decline of the capitalist social order. But though the two men agreed perfectly in recognizing the social crisis of their age, though their forecasts of the coming disaster were amazingly similar, their views of the causes of this crisis were polar opposites. And their visions of the future world to arise after the collapse of capitalism were also directly opposed.

Marx, who was influenced by Feuerbach's materialism, considered all events to be caused by material forces. Man as a psychological or a religio-moral being had no place in his system. Since he believed the inevitable decay of the Old World was being caused by economic evils, he was also convinced that future salvation lay in a just distribution of goods. Not the process of inner change in men, but transformation of external economic conditions, would bring about the millennium. According to Marx's theory of dialectical materialism, "It is not the consciousness of man which determines his existence, but on the contrary his social existence which determines his consciousness."

To Marx the spiritual and intellectual freedom of personality were of subsidiary importance. To Dostoevsky such freedom was the starting point of his social ideas. Dostoevsky, "the first great psychologist in the modern sense," who had plumbed the hidden depths of the human soul down to its religious and metaphysical source, considered economic and social conditions mere effects of spiritual and psychic causes. For him, social evils were due to "the corrupt, selfish nature of man." He was convinced that no external, material improvements, no social organizations could bring about a better world; only an inward, ethical change in man, in his instincts and way of thinking, could do that. It is with this in mind that he makes Father Zossima say in *The Brothers Karamazov*: "To transform the world, to recreate it afresh, man must turn into another path psychologically. Until you have become really, in actual fact, a brother to everyone, brotherhood will not come to pass. No sort of scientific teaching, no kind of common interest, will ever teach man to share property and privilege with equal consideration for all."

Marx's and Dostoevsky's fundamental disagreement as to which was cause and which effect resulted in diametrically opposed views of the future role of socialism. Marx considered radical socialism the only way to destroy capitalistic enslavement and eliminate all evils by organizing society on a communistic basis. And if that way were taken, he believed, chaos and doom would be converted dialectically into human happiness. Dostoevsky thought that socialism's struggle to procure economic satisfaction for the masses arose from the same fatal, materialistic spirit as the liberal-capitalist drive toward self-enrichment. He felt, therefore, that socialism would only put the finishing touch to the doom that capitalism was preparing. An inhumane communist regime would replace the inhumane capitalist one. Organized mass enslavement would appear in place of anarchic capitalist enslavement.

From Marx and Engels down to Lenin and Stalin all the communist theoreticians have given repeated assurances that dictatorial rule is only a temporary system for the period of transition, an expedient to allow for the establishment of the communist-socialist ideal state. Dostoevsky, however, foresaw the danger in the shibboleth of some future reign of happiness in whose name terrible sacrifices would be required of present-day man as his contribution toward tomorrow's man.

In the days when all brands of socialism still inscribed the ideals of fraternity and liberty on their banners, Dostoevsky predicted the emergence of the social revolution and the course it would take in the twentieth century. "They will form this organized brotherhood, and perhaps you will be one of the millions who will have to be destroyed because of it. You will be done for, for the sake of society's welfare. What is the sense of setting up an 'institution' and inscribing upon it: *'Liberté, Egalité, Fraternité'?* Nothing will come of it, so that in the end you will inevitably have to complete the phrase with *'ou la mort,'* and brothers will begin to cut each other's heads off in order to obtain brotherhood through a 'civic institution.'" Even as he saw it as inevitable, he saw this slaughter as horribly useless. "It is madness to want to bring about a new era and a new humanity by sacrificing a hundred million heads," he warned.

The conversion of the original libertarian ideals of socialism into their totalitarian opposite was not the only sign that Dostoevsky saw of the shape of things to come. Reformers and revolutionaries, liberals, socialists, and in fact most of the leading men of Dostoevsky's generation held stanchly to Comte's positivist gospel, *"Savoir pour prévoir, prévoir pour prévenir,"* and believed that with the growing enlightenment through scientific knowledge all the dark forces would be brought under control and evil would be abolished. The era had the strongest faith in "Euclidean reason." It imagined that the development of mankind would be charted in advance, like a table of logarithms, and that the future could be engineered according to clear and unassailable principles of logic.

Dostoevsky was aware, long before psychoanalysis, of the illogical forces of the unconscious, and of the lurking irrationalities in the human soul, which repeatedly overthrow all the goals set by reason. He had a foreboding of how these blind, irrational forces were destined to shape history. "They will break through all logical safeguards," he warned; "they will tear down the temple created by secular reason, and will seize control for themselves." Recent history has shown what happens when these forces take over.

Saint–Simon's cheerful conviction that "now humanity knows it is progressing" expressed the dominant tone of Dostoevsky's era, which was buoyed up by a boundless optimism. But where Saint–Simon's age saw the "dawn of civilization," Dostoevsky saw "the setting sun of the last day of civilization." In a time when all signs indicated that thanks to scientific, technological, and cultural achievements Europe was approaching its zenith, Dostoevsky wrote: "Europe is on the eve of collapse, of a terrible, universal catastrophe. . . ." And in *A Raw Youth* Versilov cries out: "One seems to hear the death knell ringing. . . . I knew that all would pass away, the whole face of the old world of Europe—sooner or later, but inevitably."

Dostoevsky was not alone in his nonconformism. There were others like him who did not have the secular faith of his age in the omnipotence of reason, in the material progress and the glorious future of European civilization. Along with him there were a few isolated writers and philosophers who felt dark forebodings and announced the impending doom. Like Marx and Dostoevsky, these other latter-day prophets were life's stepchildren, isolated personalities oppressed by illness and poverty, poor wretches among those who dwelt in comfort, malcontents among a complacent multitude.

As early as the 1840's the Danish philosopher Soeren Kierkegaard—a marked man, physically and psychically—sensed the impending spiritual crisis. He warned: "Western civilization is approaching the end of an age, and must either pass through a new religious mutation or lead to the total spiritual bankruptcy of Europe."

Almost at the same time the stricken Gogol cried out: 'Civilization has been abandoned by God and taken over by diabolic forces. It is steering toward a dreadful catastrophe."

Baudelaire's incurable illness often prevented him from knowing the date and the time of day, but it gave him in exchange knowledge of the future. He predicted: "Culture is coming to an end. . . . The time is approaching when humanity, like a vengeful cannibal, will snatch away the last portion from those who think themselves the legal heirs of the enlightened revolution. And not only political institutions, but the very fundaments of civilization itself, all its premises and preconditions, are falling to pieces. The collapse will come about through the baseness of the heart."

The sick and restless wanderer Friedrich Nietzsche, who called himself a "bird of prophecy," recognized that "our whole European culture is bound to a rack. . . . What is coming—what cannot help coming—is the onrush of nihilism."

Nevertheless Dostoevsky holds a special position among the *poetae vates* of modern time. He saw into the future in the most explicit terms, and with his dramatic genius embodied his vision in vivid episodes and in the clash of characters. The underlying theme of his novels is the crisis of our civilization. We have been through the horrors Dostoevsky described in his novels, horrors which must have seemed to the people of his far happier age the wild contrivances of a "cruel imagination." He portrayed political types that are familiar to us today; in the '70's of the last century they were considered bizarre caricatures. He virtually invented the prototypes of many of our modern political "heroes." The passionate discussions of his characters are so amazingly timely that we are almost tricked into believing these dialogues are actual and contemporary: the illusion is maintained even in phraseology and intonation. Often the novels seem to bear the same relation to the historical drama of our day that a director's script bears to the performance of a play.

Despite his uncanny keenness where the future was concerned, Dostoevsky in his role of publicist was snarled up in the current Russian political controversies. And in that field he was far from prescient and by no means free from bias.

The duality of his nature, the dichotomy that made Dostoevsky himself a "double," crops up in his sometimes disconcerting political and social attitudes. Here his vacillation between contradictory impulses, between the highest and the vilest emotions, shows up even more crudely than in his life. His concept of an evangelical, universal love was often marred by an atavistic anti-Semitism and a chauvinistic hatred of the Poles. His bigoted orthodox hostility to the Catholic Church led him to overlook the evangelical testimony of its great saints and the magnificent doctrinal systems of the Catholic theologians. He dismissed the Roman Church as the church of the Inquisition. His political allegiance with the Slavophiles made him denounce and deride, with fanatical hatred, some of the greatest ideals that Western socialism held in the past and fights for today. Whenever he took up concrete problems of European affairs, he was, as Merechkovsky remarked, "full of an un-Christian intolerance and animosity toward the unholy West."

Whenever the publicist in Dostoevsky overcame the prophet, political passion and emotional bias clouded his political visions of the future. But wherever Dostoevsky the artist couched his ideas in terms of dramatic events, of characters and fictional scenes, his creativeness made correction for the errors of his strange and contradictory character. Where the oracular publicist bungled, the visionary artist saw the future with utter distinctness.

The Possessed explores the theoretical and practical consequences of a communistic attempt to better man's lot by revolution. The author puts into the mouth of his revolutionary activist Verhovensky these words: "All reforms and improvements are nonsense and time-consuming gossip. The more we reform and improve, the worse things are; for that is only a way of artificially keeping alive something that must unconditionally collapse and die. The sooner this collapse comes, the earlier it begins, the better it will be."

In 1889, not twenty years later, this idea was taken up and amplified by the student Vladimir Ilyitch Ulianov—who was later to become, under the name of Lenin, the leader of the first successful revolution. Famine was threatening the lives of hundreds of thousands of people in Samara. During a conference of the Samara welfare committee, Lenin stood up and, like Verhovensky, warned against "the senselessness, in fact the crime," of wanting to help the hungry. For every measure to alleviate the prevailing misery, every improvement of the situation, he argued, represented a prop to the existing order, and thereby a postponement of the great collapse which alone could effect a reaction toward betterment. "The greater the need, the worse the situation," he emphasized, "the closer the disaster of the old order, the closer too is our own goal."

Verhovensky says in *The Possessed*: "The people will set up the future society *after* the destruction. Every great cause must begin with destruction. I know that, and so I am beginning!"

And Lenin used almost the same words when he began smashing the existing social order: "Only after the destruction will the future, better society be created by the people."

"What is really original and wholly your own in your conception," Razumihin says to Raskolnikov in *Crime and Punishment*, "is that, to my horror, you sanction bloodshed in the name of the idea, and with savage fanaticism in the bargain."

Verhovensky adapts Raskolnikov's individualistic justification of bloodshed to his far-flung plans for social reform. "They shout 'a hundred million heads'; that may be only a metaphor, but why be afraid of it? . . . We believe that our program is correct; that is the reason we have decided on blood."

"Our so-called revolutionaries," Lenin remarked, replying to the criticism that the Russian Civil War was costing so many lives, "imagine that we can have a revolution in the friendliest and kindliest manner—without executions. Why should we be squeamish about the sacrifices to our righteous cause? . . . It does not matter if three-quarters of mankind is destroyed; all that counts is that ultimately the last quarter should become Communist. . . . Later centuries will justify the cruelties to which circumstances have forced us. Then everything will be understood, everything."

In *The Possessed* Shigalov, the intellectual initiator of the revolutionary program Verhovensky puts into action, explains: "Dedicating my energies to the study of the social organization which is in the future to replace the present condition of things, I've come to the conviction that all makers of social systems, from ancient times up to the present year, have been dreamers, tellers of fairy tales, fools who contradicted themselves, who understood nothing of natural science and the strange animal called man. . . . But now that we are all at last preparing to act, a new form of social organization is essential. In order to avoid further uncertainty, I propose my own system of world organization. . . . My conclusion is a direct contradiction of the original idea from which I start. Starting from unlimited freedom,

I arrive at unlimited despotism. I will add, however, that there can be no solution of the social problem but mine." And Verhovensky concurs: "There has never been either freedom or equality without despotism."

Historically, socialism started with the idea of unlimited freedom for all, only to end with communism and its dictatorship. Lenin stated it well: "Freedom is a bourgeois prejudice." And arguing for the necessity of dictatorial rule, he added: "This is a principle I cling to no matter how they try to arouse the masses against my antidemocratic attitude."

Shigalov proposes dividing mankind into two unequal parts. "One-tenth enjoys absolute liberty and unbounded power over the other nine-tenths. These nine-tenths of mankind have to give up all individuality and become, so to speak, a herd," Shigalov proclaims. And Verhovensky says: "In the herd there is bound to be equality, and that's Shigalovism."

Shigalov, who justifies despotism and the depersonalization of the masses, is called in *The Possessed* "a fanatic lover of humanity." This term applies also to Lenin, whose aim was to free mankind from bondage to poverty and misery. But for all the purity of his ultimate motives, Lenin was infected with the spirit of coerciveness. Both by word and deed he revealed his underlying conviction that man had to be forcibly regimented in order to be benefited.

The dictatorial technique for depersonalizing man, as practiced so effectively in our time, already had its place in Verhovensky's program of action. Verhovensky called for "submission above all," and he visualized a future in which scientists, poets and artists would renounce their independent judgment and follow the party line rather than their own conscience or convictions. "We'll reduce all to a common denominator," he predicted. "Absolute submission, absolute loss of individuality, will result in complete equality. . . . Well, and then of course there's the main force—the cement that binds everything together will be the fear of having any opinion of one's own. That's a force for you!"

Visualizing a world in which the primacy of the party replaces all personal bonds, Versilov came to the conclusion that family ties and love, in which the personal life is most deeply rooted, were the greatest obstacles to the reduction of men to a herd. "We will destroy those desires," he says with assurance.

"Shigalov is a man of genius!" Verhovensky says. "He has invented a new system of spying. Every member of the society spies on the others, and it's his duty to inform against them."

Shigalov's ingenious scheme has made history.

"Ah, what a pity there's no proletariat! But there will be, there will!" Verhovensky promises. Lenin made good this promise.

It is almost as if events from the very beginning have modeled themselves after the pattern of Dostoevsky's prophetic novels. Verhovensky predicts: "We are going to make such an upheaval that everything will be uprooted from its foundation. . . . There's going to be an upset such as the world has never seen before. . . . The earth will weep for its old gods. . . . We are beginning with groups of five. Each of these centers of activity, proselytizing and ramifying endlessly, aims by systematic denunciation to injure the prestige of local authority, to reduce whole townships to confusion, to spread cynicism, together with complete disbelief in everything and an eagerness for revolt."

Even the fellow travelers and sympathizers are not absent from Dostoevsky's accurate forecast of a revolutionary movement that would spread over the world. "Listen," says Verhovensky, "I've reckoned them all up: A teacher who laughs with children at their God, is ours. Ours are officials and intellectuals. We have lots and lots, and they don't know it themselves."

Some of Verhovensky's statements sound uncannily like an explanation of the technique by which the free, democratic countries behind the iron curtain have been transformed into "people's democracies." For example: "In turbulent times of upheaval or transition low characters always come to the fore everywhere. I am speaking only of the riffraff which rises to the surface, whose chief aim is to find some release for its uneasiness and impatience. This riffraff almost always falls unconsciously under the control of a little group of people who do act with a definite aim, and this little group can direct all this rabble as it pleases.

. . . The most worthless fellows will suddenly gain predominant influence. They loudly criticize everything sacred, though till then they had not dared to open their mouths."

Dostoevsky knew that faith or lack of faith is the determining cultural factor behind the psychological and ideological conduct of both the individual and the masses. He knew this would be so under any social system. And accordingly he predicted that the revolutionary movement of the future would make atheism its slogan.

"Of course the first thing that must be destroyed is God," Verhovensky remarks, when he describes the development of his action program for the achievement of a new world order. This is an idea which Dostoevsky reiterated in even stronger form when he had the primal representative of atheism—the Devil—appear in the flesh to Ivan Karamazov. "I maintain that nothing need be destroyed, that we need only to destroy the idea of God in man," the Devil instructs him. "That's how we have to set to work. As soon as men, all of them, have denied God—and I believe that period, analogous with geological periods, will come to pass— the old concept of the universe will fall of itself and everything will begin anew."

Dostoevsky even developed the militant character of the coming unbeliever who sees God as a personal foe. "When one of us Russians becomes an atheist," remarks Prince Myshkin in *The Idiot,* "he will at once demand outright that the belief in God be exterminated by force."

"It would be the worst possible mistake," Lenin wrote, "for Marxists to imagine that the great millions of the people can be liberated from their intellectual darkness and ignorance merely by the direct road of Marxist enlightenment. The Marxist must be a materialist, i.e., an enemy of religion. The masses must be provided with a great variety of atheist propaganda; they must be familiarized with scientifically assembled facts; they must be approached now in one way, now in another. . . . Atheism is an integral part of the Revolution. We must fight against religion. We must overthrow God, the arch enemy of the communist order.

Deny God," he suggests, "and you can remake society on the lines of justice and equality." And he wrote to Gorky in connection with a literary controversy on *The Possessed*: "Anyone who spends his time creating God, or even merely permits such creation, demeans himself in the vilest way, for he devotes his energies to something other than action. Such a person 'lovingly contemplates' the most unsavory, the most stupid, the most slavish aspects of life. From the social point of view all God-seeking and God-making is nothing but smug self-contemplation of the stupid *petit bourgeois,* the brittle philistine, the dreamy, self-deprecating little bourgeois who is 'desperate and tired.' . . ."

In *The Possessed* Dostoevsky takes up the theory of reform by coercion only as it operates at its outset, when it is still but a program and a party. In the *Legend of the Grand Inquisitor* he portrays its finished product, an ironclad Utopia.

Why does Dostoevsky put his prophecies of the coming social order into the mouth of a legendary medieval grand inquisitor? This is understandable only if we remember Dostoevsky's anti-Catholic bias. He saw Catholicism, with its Inquisition and its excursions into power politics, as a betrayal of Christ; he suspected Roman Catholicism of being an elaborate screen concealing a secret godlessness. And so he has the grand inquisitor reveal that he is not in league with the Saviour, but with His antagonist, the Devil. Like the characters in *The Possessed,* the grand inquisitor announces that mankind will be made happy by a coercive organization that despises man. The idea is the direct opposite of Christ's doctrine that God upholds the freedom of man's personality.

Nicolai Berdyayev, one of the most reliable interpreters of Dostoevsky's thought, believes that in his grand inquisitor Dostoevsky was symbolizing communistic socialism rather than theocratic Catholicism. Berdyayev points out the amazing parallels between the ideas of the inquisitor and those of Shigalov and Verhovensky. Another thing to consider is that the idea of earthly weal through material security—the grand inquisitor's slogan of "bread"—has little or nothing to do with the spirit of medievalism. which preached in terms of Heaven and Hell of the hereafter. Posthumous writings of Dostoevsky, discovered after Berdyayev wrote, also tend to confirm Berdyayev's thesis. The regime administered by the grand inquisitor is probably not the medieval church, but a future communist "paradise."

In *The Legend of the Grand Inquisitor,* then, the paradox of the communist program is examined down to its ultimate causes and effects. Here we are introduced to the fascinating, complex psychology of the benevolent dictator who is set on reforming the world by force. The grand inquisitor is a Shigalov sublimated and ennobled. Through him we are better able to comprehend the fanaticism of a Lenin. Both show the same "compelling logic," the same iron will in bringing about the realization of a plan. Like the grand inquisitor, Lenin was one of those "patient sufferers who are consumed by a terrible sorrow and who love humanity." Like the grand inquisitor, Lenin had a deep sympathy for the oppressed masses, at the same time that he exercised a ruthless contempt for the dignity of the individual. He was an ascetic who harbored no material interests. He was an idealist; and even a hero for his cause, bravely facing suffering. Yet he could not design a better order without enslaving a whole people.

In the grand inquisitor's defense of his work for humanity, Dostoevsky makes a point which the history of our times has underlined. "Oh, we will persuade men that they can never be free until they renounce their freedom in our favor and bow down to us. And in the end they will understand at last that freedom and bread enough for all are inconceivable together, for never, never will they be able to share between them." And bolshevism proclaimed: "Only by firm control can there be achieved the perfect social order in which there is an equal and just distribution of food." The masses were promised bread in exchange for the surrender of their freedom.

Seventy years ago Dostoevsky's fictional character Arcady (*A Raw Youth*) asked a group of young revolutionaries the same skeptical question that many who are outside the iron curtain are asking the missionaries of this new world order: "Tell me what inducement you hold out to me to follow you?" he asks. "How do you prove to me that you will make things better? How will you deal with my individual protest in your barracks? You will have barracks, communistic homes, *stricte necessaire,* atheism—that's your ideal. I know all about it. And for all this, for this little part of mediocre advantage, for a bit of bread and a warm corner, you will take away all my personal liberty, my personality."

Raskolnikov, condemned to Siberia, has a fevered dream in which he beholds the world of the future—our world—swept by an ideological plague. "He dreamt that the whole world was condemned to a terrible, new, strange plague that had come to Europe from the depths of Asia. Some new sort of microbes were attacking the bodies of men, but these microbes were endowed with intelligence and will. Men attacked by them became the victims of fantastic delusions. But never had men considered themselves so intellectual and so completely in possession of the truth as these sufferers, never had they considered their decisions, their scientific conclusions, their moral convictions so infallible. Whole villages, towns and peoples went mad from the infection. All men and all things were involved in the destructiveness. And men killed each other in a sort of senseless spite."

Dostoevsky foresaw not only the distortion of the humanist ideals of socialism, but he predicted also another trend of our times—the rise of antihumanist irrationalism. Here again he employs monologues, dialogues, and dramatic scenes to drive home his ideas.

In *Notes from Underground,* where the revolt against reason is embodied in the figure of the underground man, Dostoevsky wrote: "In accordance with the irrational traits of his [the underground man's] nature, he will shatter every system which has ever been established by lovers of the human race for the race's improvement. He will cut straight across both the dictates of reason and his own 'true interest' and everything else. Out of sheer devilment he will do the most senseless things for the sole purpose that he may alloy all the solemn good sense that has been lavished upon him. And if he could not get his way he would then proceed to introduce chaos and disruption into everything, and to devise enormities of all kinds. If the need should arise he would be ready to contravene every law, and to lose sight alike of honor and peace. And if reason should try to play havoc with his plans, well, in that case I believe he would purposely become a lunatic, in order to become devoid of reason and therefore able to insist upon himself."

⌐   And in the same book Dostoevsky made this amazing prophecy: "I should not be surprised if amid all this order and regularity of the future there should suddenly arise some common-faced or rather cynical and sneering gentleman who, with his arms akimbo, will say to us: 'Now then, you fellows, what about smashing to smithereens all this solemn reason and beginning to live our own lives again according to our own sweet will?' "

Sixty years later this very figure appeared in the flesh on the Piazza Venezia, seventy years later in Nuremberg. "Let's junk everything that the faith in reason ever produced!" Mussolini proclaimed. To a world that even after World War I cherished the hope that the society of the future could be organized along rational lines, he opposed his faith in the *anima appassionata* of the force of will.

⌐   "The century of reason is over. I hate everything that comes from mind and humanitarianism. The intellect is suspect; place all your trust in the instincts," Hitler declared. And in the place of the ideal of reason he set the new myth of the "glory of the blood."

⌐   *Notes from Underground* contains a thumbnail sketch of this "devotee of irrationalism" that sounds like the analysis by some thoughtful newspaper correspondent of the era of fascism and national socialism. "All men of independence and action . . . are both gross and limited in their point of view. Such men are led by their limitations to mistake approximate and secondary causes for primary ones, and so to persuade themselves that they have an assured basis for their actions and therefore have nothing to worry about. To embark upon action one must first of all feel perfectly sure of oneself, so that no doubts as to the wisdom of action may arise."

At a time when the liberal nineteenth century considered

material welfare the chief criterion of life, the underground man stated: "There is something which is dearer to man than his economic interests, something that is stronger than all his other interests put together. He will gladly forgo happiness, security, and even wealth, and set off on a risky road as though he preferred to essay the difficult and awkward path along which he must feel his way in darkness. . . . Mayn't it be that he also loves adversity? Certainly there are times when man *does* love adversity, love it passionately. And may not adversity be as good for him as happiness? An occasional catastrophe, come weal come woe, seems to me a very pleasant thing."

Mussolini held the same ideas: "Our battle is an ungrateful one, yet it is a beautiful battle, since it compels us to count only on our own forces," he declared. "Revealed truth we have torn to shreds, dogmas we have spat upon, we have rejected all theories of paradise, we have banished charlatans, white, red, black charlatans who place miraculous drugs on the market to give 'happiness' to mankind. We do not believe in programs, in plans, in saints or apostles; above all we do not believe in happiness, in salvation, in the promised land. . . . We do not believe in the concept of happiness of the humanistic sheep. Theirs is a puny, contemptible goal."

Versilov in *A Raw Youth* puts forward a thesis which at the time must have puzzled the middle-class citizen whose chief interest was bettering his position. "I don't want to seduce you from your ideals, to tempt you in the direction of bourgeois virtue," he says to Arcady. "I am not assuring you that 'happiness is better than heroism'; on the contrary, 'heroism is finer than any happiness.' That's a settled thing between us."

Twenty years later there appeared the apostles Sorel and Nietzsche, who made a creed out of this dangerous and heroic concept of life. Sorel proclaimed the myth of heroism and violence as essential to any creative historical movement. He called for "a great war which would reinvigorate men's energies; in any case, would doubtless bring to power men with the will to govern; or a great extension of violence, which would place the middle classes face to face with revolutionary reality and make them sick of humanitarian platitudes." And Nietzsche asserted that struggle and insecurity constituted the "dignity" of the new man.

Mussolini, who prepared for the role of fascist leader by steeping himself in the theories of these two philosophers, affirmed his faith in "everything that means danger and insecurity." He stated explicitly: "We do not care for progress, but rather for the dangerous, heroic life, for the daring deed, in which alone this age can fulfill itself."

As Dostoevsky foresaw the revolutionary brand of socialism without knowing Marx, so also he anticipated the doctrines of Nietzsche. One might say that he delineated not only Nietzsche's philosophy, but even many features of the man himself in the person of Kirillov in *The Possessed*. The role Nietzsche played in the drama of European intellectual history was so close to the role of Kirillov that it was as if he were carrying out a preordained assignment. Nietzsche proclaimed that everything was lawful. In exultant dithyrambs he heralded the metamorphosis of man into superman, the man-god.

At the time that Dostoevsky was expounding in *Crime and Punishment* the privileges of the superman, Nietzsche was a young theological student. At the time that Dostoevsky was forging the character of Kirillov, Nietzsche was twenty-four, had switched to the study of classical philology, and was teaching at Basle. It was another ten years before he wrote *Zarathustra;* and his *The Will to Power* was not published until after Dostoevsky's death.

It is in Dostoevsky that we find the first enunciation of the idea of "the will to power." Not only did he present these principles, but he comprehended to what they would lead. "Power is a sign of strength, and strength is the token of the great and extraordinary man," Dostoevsky wrote in a draft of *Crime and Punishment*. And Raskolnikov says to Sonya: "Anyone who is greatly daring is right in men's eyes, and he who dares most of all will be most in the right."

Decades later Nietzsche wrote: "What is good always elevates the sense of power, the will to power, and power itself in

man. . . . Man must be like the lion, who says, 'I will!' and
tramples to pieces everything that gets in his way."

Nietzsche's new type of man, mad for power and imbued
with a Raskolnikov's fanaticism of the will, turned up in the figure
of Mussolini. "This age can be shaped only by will power," the
Duce cried out. "Yes, I am possessed by the fever of the will; it
burns me, wears me down, devours me inwardly like a physical
pain. I want to scratch with my will, scratch a mark on the age
like a lion with his paw." And trampling down everything that
stood in his way, he created the new order of fascism, governed
by his authoritarian will.

In a telegram of congratulation sent to the Duce on his
fiftieth birthday, the Weimar Nietzsche Institute hailed Mussolini
as "the inspired rejuvenator of the Nietzschean spirit . . . the
grandest disciple of Zarathustra Nietzsche could ever have
dreamed of."

The Third Reich adopted Nietzsche's aspirations as its own,
and Hitler set himself up as the Nietzschean ideal leader, "clad
in the armor of hardness," and "free of the meekness and degen-
eracy of Christianity."

"I believe in my leading idea," Raskolnikov stated in his
article *On Crime,* "that men are divided by a law of nature into
two categories: inferior (ordinary), that is to say, a material that
serves only to reproduce its kind; and men who have the gift or
the talent to utter *a new word,* and are destined to rule over
the others."

So it was the student Raskolnikov who first voiced the theory
of the superman who stands above morality. Nietzsche turned this
idea into a philosophical concept. And Hitler was to set up a
regime based on this theory, a regime which was a scourge for
millions. Carrying his principle into international politics, he
announced: "The superior race subjugates the inferior race. This
frequently leads to the subjection of a number of nations to the
will of only a few men, a subjugation that rests simply on the
might of the stronger."

"Ordinary men have to live in submission; have no right to

transgress the law, because they are ordinary. But extraordinary men have a right to transgress the law, just because they are extraordinary. . . . If such a one is forced for the sake of his idea to step over a corpse or wade through blood, he can find in himself, in his conscience, a sanction for wading through blood—note that. Everything is lawful to the real master." This was Raskolnikov's theory of antimorality, and it anticipated Nietzsche in replacing the old "tables of values" by new principles "beyond good and evil."

"Those who are responsible to history must be as free as God," Hitler declared, making this doctrine his and acting accordingly. "Their sole and highest goal in all they do is to hold their power. Certainly our path is not stainless. But I know of no single case in which a man has taken the road to power without wading through the mire."

Raskolnikov, though he considered himself a superman, confined his "principled" murder to the destruction of a single "inferior, worthless life." Hitler, acting on the historic scale, snuffed out millions of precious lives "on principle," for the sake of his idea.

Communism arises from the spirit of materialist rationalism; fascism and national socialism from mythic irrationalism. Communism set as its ultimate goal collective man; fascism the heroic colossus of the superstate; and national socialism the Aryan superman.

Different as these movements may be in origin and aims, they have confronted our age with a unitary historical phenomenon: the totalitarian regime. In our times totalitarianism is of fateful importance to the whole of human civilization; in Dostoevsky's time it existed neither as a historical fact nor as an intellectual possibility.

The secular Enlightenment which replaced divine will by the rule of reason, though it discarded religious dogma nevertheless presupposed that the basic ethical ideals of Christianity were inviolable goods. The religious idea that the human race is united by brotherly love became in secular form the ideal of unity through the tolerance, community of interests, and peaceful compromise. The religious belief that all men are children of God was perpetuated in the democratic ideology in the thesis that all citizens possess the same rights and obligations.

Totalitarianism is the denial of all these ideals. Totalitarianism destroys both the religious and the humanistic belief in the unity of the human race. Communism separated humanity into two hostile classes. Fascism boasted that it had set up "creative and wholesome inequalities." Nazism founded its ideology on the theoretical distinction between "superior" and "inferior" races. Totalitarianism of the left and of the right denies the primacy of the personality. Communism reduces man to the "aggregate of collective conditions," fascism to "building material of the national superstate," national socialism to a "cell in the racial body." All three are alike in eliminating the freedom of the individual—communism in the name of the higher interests of the collective group, fascism in the name of national greatness, national socialism in the name of purity of the race. Lenin, with cold, rationalistic objectivity, dismissed freedom as a bourgeois prejudice; Mussolini shouted with Roman pomposity: "I am determined to stride unhesitatingly over the deformed body of the goddess of liberty." And Hitler proclaimed with *furor teutonicus*: "Terrorism is indispensable. . . . Every regime is at bottom tyranny and cannot help being. . . . It is inconceivable that government and order can be preserved without coercion." Unanimously they rejected tolerance and peaceful agreement, and made totalitarian intolerance the principle of their new orders. *"Écraser!"* Lenin cried, whenever anything or anyone would not fit into his plan. "The fascist state is all-embracing; outside of it no human and spiritual values can exist," Mussolini proclaimed. "World views admit no compromise. National socialism insists upon merciless racial reconstitution of the whole of life according to its views," Hitler declared. The communist "party line," the fascist "discipline," the German *"Gleichschaltung,"* leveled everything, coordinated everything.

"Like a clenched fist, Lenin's inextinguishable hatred was held out against the bourgeoisie," Lenin's comrade and friend Zinoviev declared, "and just as he knew only hatred for his political adversaries, so the hateful shouts of his opponents were 'music to his ears.' " In the mausoleum on Red Square, which has become a place of pilgrimage, Lenin's embalmed corpse lies on its glass bier with clenched fist, even in death. Lenin preached "creative hatred," Mussolini "the transforming struggle," and Hitler "exterminating race hate."

"What will prevail is violence erupting from the primal cause and creating a new world and new social orders," said Sorel, the harbinger of the "gospel without pity." And before his death *Père* Sorel hailed Lenin, "who is creating the world anew by violence." Sorel also saluted the young Mussolini as "the hero of the future"; he called Mussolini's first literary effort "a philosophy of violence," and later described Mussolini's fascism as "born in the labor of struggle and violence." Nietzsche's phrase, "Praised be whatever makes us hard!" served Hitler as the motto of his Aryan racial state.

Oppression, hatred, and violence have of course existed in earlier periods of history. But nineteenth-century humanism had been looking forward to a rational social order that would eliminate those evils; a future based on the opposite of all its hopes and efforts seemed inconceivable to the nineteenth century. And it was even more inconceivable that potential despots could induce the masses to obey them willingly, that the masses could see their own oppression as the sole road to salvation, could accept their rulers' doctrine that individual freedom is incompatible with the common welfare, and could interpret depersonalization as a blessing for both the individual and the generality.

Thus the mentality of modern totalitarianism, of both the rulers and the victims, was utterly alien to the thought of the nineteenth century. Dostoevsky alone foresaw the hidden roots and the ugliest excrescences of that mentality, and prophetically described them in his works.

Dostoevsky's allegory of the grand inquisitor offers a masterful insight into the psychology of the modern totalitarian state, in all its paradoxical complexity. "There is no equality without a tyrant to guarantee it, and no tyranny that does not result in the equalization of all by oppression," the grand inquisitor proclaims. And indeed, dictatorship and collectivity are prerequisites of one another; each produces the other out of itself.

The grand inquisitor also supplies us with an answer to the enigma of millions of human-beings voluntarily, or even gladly, giving up their freedom and submitting to dictatorship. Almost seventy years ago Dostoevsky's medieval grand inquisitor acted with a knowledge of the juxtaposition of leader fascination and collective psyche that puts into the shade our laborious modern theories of mass psychology.

The grand inquisitor accuses Christ, Who has returned to earth and been clapped into prison by the inquisitor's orders, of having burdened man by giving him freedom to choose between good and evil, truth and falsehood. The gift is a responsibility far beyond man's powers. "Nothing is more seductive for man than his freedom of conscience," he says, "but nothing is a greater cause of suffering. . . . Man is tormented by no greater anxiety than to find someone quickly to whom he can hand over that gift of freedom with which the ill-fated creature is born." And describing the dictator worship of the masses, he continues: "They will be awestricken before us, and will be proud at our being so powerful and clever that we have been able to subdue such a turbulent flock of millions. They will tremble impotently before our wrath, but they will be just as ready at a sign from us to pass to laughter and rejoicing. . . . They will marvel at us and look on us as gods, because we are ready to endure the freedom which they have found so dreadful, and to rule over them. . . . Yes, we shall have an answer for all. And they will be glad to believe our answer, for it will save them from the great anxiety and terrible agony they endure in making a free decision for themselves."

"Providence has destined me to be the greatest liberator of mankind," Hitler once remarked. "I free man from the fetters of a filthy and humiliating self-torture, the chimera called conscience; and from the requirements of freedom and personal independence, which only very few are able to endure. The leader-lawgiver frees the mass of believers from the burden of free will."

"We have a right to teach men that it is not the free judgment of their hearts, not love that matters, but a mystery which they must follow blindly, even against their conscience," the grand inquisitor says. Convinced of this, he has appropriated "the authority of infallibility which alone keeps and grants the mystery of good and evil."

In similar fashion modern dictators claimed the authority of infallibility; on this basis they could demand that men obey not individual conscience, but the dictates of party leaders, who alone have the right to decide what is useful or harmful to the majority. "I have no conscience," Goering stated. "My conscience is Adolf Hitler." In Italy Mussolini shouldered the burden of the fascists' conscience. And in Russia Stalin has replaced Lenin in being the conscience of every loyal member of the Communist Party.

"So long as man remains free," says the grand inquisitor, "he strives for nothing so incessantly and so painfully as to find someone to worship. . . . And they are concerned not only to find what one or the other can worship, but to find something that all would believe in and worship." "A new religion is coming instead of an old one," Dostoevsky proclaims in *A Raw Youth*, thereby foreseeing the fanatical core of the totalitarian movements, the religious motivation underneath the wrappings of scientific Marxism and Nietzschean philosophy.

In another passage in *A Raw Youth* Dostoevsky says: "When man rejects God he bows instead to an idol. . . . They are all idolizers." All totalitarian movements bear witness to this fact; in them the cult of the dictator has replaced the cult of God. This fully corresponds to the world which Ivan's devil predicted as resulting from the new religion of the here and now. "Man will be lifted up with a spirit of divine Titanic pride," the Devil tells Ivan Karamazov, "and the man-god will appear." By the apocalyptic vision of the man-god Dostoevsky meant the spiritual antagonist of Christ, the Antichrist who will come to deny the teachings of Christ, the God-man. Rejecting man's spiritual destiny, the man-god preaches goals purely of this world. He sets men to striving exclusively for economic reform, for the superstate, or for racial purity, and to trying for happiness by physical violence.

Dostoevsky foresaw fully the anti-Christian spirit behind the new religions of our age: dialectical materialism, Italian Caesarism, and Germanic racialism. In this sense Stavrogin remarks to Shatov in *The Possesssed*: "Verhovensky is convinced that Christianity is not only absolutely unnecessary for men, but that it is positively harmful; and that if they completely exterminate Christianity mankind will at once blossom into the true new life. His terrible power lies in that belief."

To exterminate Christianity so that mankind will blossom into the true new life became the goal of all totalitarian regimes. This was the aim behind the agitation of the Comsomols, the young communists who under Lenin practiced "red prayers" and "red masses" to mock at Christianity. The same aim is back of the present religious persecutions behind the iron curtain. In Italy Mussolini acted the shrewd diplomat and paid lip service to Christianity, but as a disciple of Nietzsche's religion of the strong he saw to it that fascism practiced Nietzsche's contempt for Christian principles.

With the fanatical conviction that the blessing of the ancient Teutonic war gods rested on his chosen head, Hitler decreed: "Instead of the blood of a so-called Saviour, the Germans will worship the pure blood of our race." And his apostle Rosenberg wrote: "The Christian religion is a hindrance to the organic forces of the Nordic racially determined peoples and must give way to them. For Christianity demands primarily love in the sense of humility, mercy, submission, and asceticism. Today it is clear to every honest German that this doctrine of love embracing equally all the creatures in the world is a severe blow to the soul of the Nordic man."

It was Dostoevsky's conviction that this new religion of the here and now would wipe out all the "tables of law," would obliterate transcendental Christian-Occidental morality. Sooner or later, he knew, the man who had forsworn all allegiance to divine commandments would exchange absolute values for ephemeral advantages.

The grand inquisitor says to Christ, Who represents the eternal and absolute laws: "Dost Thou know that the ages will pass, and humanity will proclaim by the lips of their sages, that there is no crime, and therefore no sin; there is only hunger? 'Feed men and then ask of them virtue!' that's what they'll write on their banner, which they will raise against Thee, and with which they will destroy Thy temple."

It has happened even as the grand inquisitor predicted. The Marxist doctrinaires came and declared that hunger was the cause of all crime, and that what had been known as virtue was just the ideological superstructure of economic conditions. And the communist revolution, its banners proclaiming that economic necessities come before moral commandments, rose in revolt against the teachings of Christ. Lenin proclaimed: "We repudiate all morality that proceeds from supernatural ideas that are outside of class conception. In our opinion morality is entirely subordinate to the interest of the class struggle. We do not believe in eternal principles of morality, and we will expose this deception. Communist morality is identical with the fight for the strengthening of the dictatorship of the proletariat." And another time Lenin said: "Dictatorship is an authority relying directly upon force and not bound by any laws. The revolutionary dictatorship of the proletariat is an authority maintained by means of force over and against the bourgeoisie and not bound by any law."

E. Preobrazhenski, Stalin's predecessor as secretary of the Communist Party, who faithfully recorded all the "moral and class norms" Lenin ever advocated, summarized the problem of morality as the bolsheviks saw it. "Translated from the misty language of ethics into that of ordinary life, morality means what is advantageous, useful, and expedient for a definite group of people; on the other hand, the immoral is whatever the same group considers injudicious or inexpedient. Therefore the attitude of the working class and the Communist Party to the open recognition of the right to lie is quite different from that of the Western European Socialists, those God-fearing *petits bourgeois*."

When in the early days of the communist movement Lenin was accused of admitting members into the party without making any moral discrimination, he retorted: "The party is not a dormitory for noble maidens. We cannot approach our active members with a narrow bourgeois yardstick. . . . On the barricades a safeblower will be more useful than Plekhanov."

Mussolini placed himself "beyond good and evil," and shaped his "ethical" concepts accordingly.

Hitler, in his onslaught against Christian principles, endorsed only a biological morality; his point of reference was the religion of race. What was good or bad, what true or false, was determined on racial principles. "There is no absolute moral truth," Hitler declared. "I recognize no moral law. It is the duty of Germans not to seek objective truth where it may be favorable to others, but to work tirelessly for their own truths. . . . Undoubtedly I have an advantage over the bourgeois democrats, for I am free of pedantic and sentimental inhibitions. Am I to renounce this advantage merely because my opponents have not advanced so far? I am ready to use any method of cheating and deception if it serves my ideas. Every act, even crime, has its place. The ten commandments have lost all applicability." And he admitted to Rauschnig: "I have made it my business to study human weaknesses. We would do well to speculate on human vice instead of human virtues. I don't shrink from making use of eccentric and abnormal people and all sorts of adventurers. There are countless people of this sort who are useless in respectable life, but who for our purposes are invaluable. We have no scruples. I expect every one of us to be a member of one family of conspirators."

If we have followed Dostoevsky's predictions so far, we have to follow him one step farther, and agree that we are all implicated in the deplorable trends of our times.

"Don't say, the power of evil, of the wicked world, is great, but we, we are guiltless. . . . We are responsible to all for all, apart from our own sins. It's only that men don't know it. . . . Each man is part of the single organism of all humanity, and every one of us accordingly shares the guilt for every crime, for everything that happens on earth." The speaker of these words is Elder Zossima of *The Brothers Karamazov*. That the last idea is one which Dostoevsky held strongly is indicated by the insistency with which he repeats it. For example, he wrote in *The Diary of a Writer*: "Salvation from evil is possible only if everyone confesses to all and sundry that he too, in fact especially he himself, is morally responsible, morally shares the guilt for everything. This is a lucid and true idea," he goes on, "which sooner or later will in any case become firmly established, and triumph."

It might once have been argued that this "lucid idea" is self-evident only to a Christian in a state of mystical exaltation. But today, after the experiences of two world wars and the resulting revolutions, the idea has a new appeal and validity. What political party, whether socialist, liberal, or conservative, what nation, what school of philosophy, can say today with good conscience: "The power of evil, of the wicked world, is great, but we, we are guiltless"?

Like so many other concepts of Dostoevsky, the idea of collective guilt was seized upon in our day. It has been taken up by Carl Jung, the psychologist of the collective unconscious, who in a recent essay treats the psychological concept of collective guilt. Jung writes: "Guilt can be narrowed down to the lawbreaker only when considered from the legal, moral, and intellectual point of view. But as a psychological phenomenon it involves everybody. . . . A crime can never happen as our own consciousness sees it, exclusively in and for itself. On the contrary, it happens in a wide radius. The wickedness of the others instantly becomes our own wickedness, because it kindles evil in our own soul. The crime has been partly suffered by everyone, and everyone has also partly committed it. . . . No one need hope to escape this fact, for everybody harbors his 'statistical' criminal in himself. . . . In order to be able at all to sever our union with evil, we really require a regular *rite de sortie*: a sort of ceremony in which the judge, the hangman, and the people would solemnly declare their guilt and their willingness to make amends. If only men could see what personal enrichment comes out of recognizing their complicity in all that happens! What a sense of honesty and what a new spiritual honor that affords!"

We have indicated that many of Dostoevsky's political prophecies have been confirmed in our own time, down to specific details. There are others which time has proved false. The best known of these—and the one that is always brought up when Dostoevsky's right to the name of prophet is questioned—is his prediction of Russia's future Christian mission. It is an interesting coincidence that the other great political prophet of the nineteenth century—Karl Marx, who like Dostoevsky forecast the future with a high degree of accuracy—also made his greatest mistake in regard to Russia.

Marx predicted that by dialectical law the social revolution would have to break out first in the highly industrialized capitalist countries of the West—England, Germany and France—and would spread out from there to conquer the world. A social revolution in technically backward, primitive, agrarian Russia scarcely occurred to Marx; in *the Communist Manifesto* he did not think Russia even worth mentioning. But in fact the Marxist revolution broke out in that very country, industrially undeveloped as it was, while capitalism held on, and is still holding, in the western countries. Moreover, the collapse of Germany did not come about as a result of the dialectical struggle between capitalism and the proletariat. A rabid nationalism that Marx never foresaw led to the Nazi revolution and the subsequent disaster. And the present labor government of England is a strong bulwark against communist revolution.

In contrast to Marx, Dostoevsky saw Russia as the land which would "introduce the new age." But his error was in believing that Russia would fulfill her future mission by an intensification of Christianity "against the rock of which atheistic communism from the West will be shattered." In fact the atheistic communist revolution broke out in that very Russia of his, and at the present time it is the West that remains the "rock."

Here again it is obvious that when Dostoevsky trusted the prophetic vision which came to him as a creative artist, he saw the future clearly. Thus in *The Idiot* Prince Myshkin predicts that the Russian atheist will march at the head of the atheist movement. And not only does Dostoevsky see in *The Possessed* the atheistic revolution which is brewing in Russia, but he has Shatov —the believer in Russia's Christian mission—murdered. And Verhovensky's revolution strides on over Shatov's corpse. But this clear insight into the future falters as soon as the Slavophile publicist and professional propagandist of nationalism becomes dominant over Dostoevsky the artist. Inspired by the wish-dream of the Orthodox Christian, and at the same time imbued with a chauvinistic love of Russia, Dostoevsky proclaimed the impending union of his nation with Messianic Christianity. He makes the Russians the "God-bearing people" whose future role will be the realization of the gospels upon earth.

"The greatest of all the great future missions of the Russians," he says in *The Diary of a Writer,* "is to pronounce the final word—the omnihuman all-unity of a brotherly communion of all nations in accordance with the laws of the Gospel of Christ. Our role in humankind is to become a servant to all nations for the sake of general pacification. Our goal is a fellowship with full respect for national individuality, for the maintenance of complete liberty of men with the indication of what liberty comprises, i.e., loving communion guaranteed by deeds, by the living example, by the factual need of brotherhood, and not by means of chopping off millions of heads."

This is a prophecy which has gone unfulfilled. History dissolved the amalgam of nationalism and religion. Russia went the way of all powers; she abandoned the political road pointed out by the religious thinker, and turned toward the atheistic dictatorship à la Shigalov and Verhovensky.

It is clear that both Dostoevsky and Marx miscalculated the future role of Russia. But Dostoevsky was only half mistaken. While Marx assigned no role at all to Russia in the shaping of the future, Dostoevsky did predict that Russia's future function would be a crucial one. This proved to be so, in a sense entirely different from the one he imagined. Yet if we assign a different symbol to his picture of Russia's part in the future—the hammer and sickle of atheistic communism instead of the Christian cross

Dostoevsky envisioned—we find that his prophecies are singularly apt.

"The future independent Russian idea has not yet been born, yet the earth is uncannily pregnant with it and is already preparing to give birth, in frightful labor, to this idea . . . ," Dostoevsky wrote as early as the eighteen-seventies. "Once we have begun to understand what we really are, we will undoubtedly utter in Europe such a word as has never been heard before." The message which Russia alone was elected to give the world was, for Dostoevsky and later for the Communists, "the idea of Russian nationalism as equivalent to the idea of universal humanity." Modern Russia has an almost religious fanaticism concerning her world mission and sends her atheistic apostles into all countries of the world to convert humanity to the Russian idea and let all men share in the Russian redemption.

"The destiny of Russia is pan-European and universal," Dostoevsky wrote. "To become a true Russian . . . means only to become a Universal Man. . . . There we have something final which, though by no means solving all human destinies, brings with it the beginning of the end of the whole former history of European mankind—the beginning of the solution of its further destinies."

Likewise, Dostoevsky's awareness of the mysterious force peculiar to Russia, and the fascination that force exercises upon the rest of the world, has been confirmed. So has his intuitive knowledge of the weakness of the West European countries and their internal flaws. Versilov, who embodies the Russian man of the future, says in *A Raw Youth*: "Europe has created a noble type of Frenchman, of Englishman, and of German, but of the man of the future she scarcely knows at present. . . . Every Frenchman can serve not only his France, but humanity, but only on condition that he remain French to the utmost possible degree, and it's the same for the Englishman and the German. Only to the Russian has been vouchsafed the capacity to become most of all Russian only when he is most European. That is the most essential difference between us Russians and all the rest, and in that respect the position of Russia is unique. I am in France a Frenchman, with a German I am a German, and by that very fact I am most typically a Russian and am most truly serving Russia, for I am bringing out her leading idea. Only Russia lives not for herself but for an idea. I am a pioneer of this idea . . . I am the custodian of the Russian future. There are, perhaps, only a thousand of us in Russia, possibly more, possibly less—but all Russia has existed, so far, only to produce that thousand."

And here again is a pronouncement uncannily appropriate for the present: "At no time could Russia have congratulated herself with more joy upon the fact that she is not the Old but the New Europe; that she is, *in se,* a separate and mighty world for which the time has now come to enter a new and superior phase of her potency, and to become more than ever independent of others, their fatal questions with which decrepit Europe has bound herself. . . . Almost with certainty it may be stated that very soon, perhaps in the immediate future, Russia will prove stronger than any nation in Europe. This will come to pass because all great powers in Europe will be destroyed for the simple reason that they will be worn out and undermined by the unsatisfied democratic tendencies of an enormous portion of their lowerclass subjects. . . . There will remain on the continent but one colossus—Russia. This will come to pass, perhaps even much sooner than people think. . . . The future of Europe belongs to Russia. But the question is: what will Russia then be doing in Europe? What role will she be playing?"

And this same anxious question is asked today by all who are concerned for the fate of western civilization.

For this Russia which is now a world power, which already rules a large part of Europe, is not the Russia that Dostoevsky as a Christian, a political publicist and a wishful thinker saw in the future. Rather, it is the Russia that Dostoevsky the creative artist prophetically described in his novels, the Russia of *The Possessed*, of Shigalov, Verhovensky and—the grand inquisitor.

Dostoevsky's prediction, however, goes beyond the time of crisis in which we are at present. He promised that in the end we

shall be saved. This is the message to be found in even the grim-
mest of Dostoevsky's novels, and the same good tidings illuminate
also the last of his prophetic visions: "It is perhaps useless to
mourn when confronted with this last struggle of the old civilization, and to shrink back from it, for we shall then be on the eve
of a great renewal which will certainly come once humanity has
made the painful journey from doubt to despair," he wrote. In
this sense he is not only the prophet of doom but the guide who
points the way out of our contemporary chaos toward a better
society and happier future.

He insists that this way could only be through a revived faith.
"I could not help wondering at times how man could live without
God, and whether that will ever be possible. My heart always
decided that it was impossible," Versilov admits in *A Raw Youth,*
after a ranting depiction of a future world without religion. "At a
certain period it might seem possible on account of what is called
'logic.' But I always imagined a different picture in the end. . . .
I picture to myself that strife has ceased. After curses, pelting
with mud, and hisses, has come a lull, and men are left alone and
at once feel terribly forlorn. Then they will again remember
Him. . . . I must complete my picture of future humanity in
this way."

The guiding force which will lead men back from un-
belief to renewed faith in God, from forlornness to renewal and
reconstruction, is according to Dostoevsky the teachings of Christ,
Who had shown by the example of His life how to attain God.

So he has Versilov say: "I could not get on without Christ.
I simply cannot imagine men without Him. Since He once was,
He can never again leave them, and if He did leave they would
find Him of themselves . . . and He would lead them to God."

For the one guarantee of true fraternal equality and justice
lies in Christ's message of love; His gospel contains the deepest
affirmation of the freedom of the individual which is implicit in
the choice between good and evil. The acceptance as a grace
of the moral burden which Christ imposed on humanity can assure
a true social commonwealth for man. The single solution to our
problem lies in recalling that political and social questions are

indivisible from the teachings of Christ. The way to a better world is a *politae Christi*. "There is no other portal to blessedness for humanity than the one which leads to His message," Dostoevsky wrote. "With Christ or without Him—these alternatives comprise the entire destiny of mankind. And the moment man once more feels the tremendous fact of Christ's constant presence in his heart, he will take the true road of ascent."

In statements such as this Dostoevsky anticipated the underlying thesis of leading contemporary thinkers, philosophers, scientists, clergymen, writers, and statesmen, all who have given thought to the way by which "doubt and despair" may be overcome, who have taken arms against existentialist hopelessness and pointed to the way out of chaos.

LIFE AND WORKS

1821	Dostoyevsky born in Moscow hospital for the poor (October 30).
1837–43	Studies at Engineering School, Petersburg.
1846	*Poor Folks, The Double.*
1849	*Netotchka Nesvanova.*
	Arrest April 23, interned at Peter and Paul Fortress. Sent to Siberia, Christmas Eve.
1850–54	Siberian Katorga at Omsk.
1857	Marries Maria Dmitrievna.
1861–62	*Insulted and Injured, The House Of The Dead.*
1863	*Notes from Underground*
1864	Wife and brother die.
1866	*Crime and Punishment. The Gambler.*
1867	Marries Anna Grigorievna.
1867–71	European exil.
1868	*The Idiot.*
1870	*The Eternal Husband.*
1871	Returns to Russia.
1872	*The Possessed.*
1875	*A Raw Youth.*
1876–77	*Diary of a Writer.*
1880	*The Brothers Karamazov.* Pushkin address.
1881	Dies in Petersburg (January 28).

SHORT BIBLIOGRAPHY

Berdyayev, Nikolas, A.: *Dostoevsky, an Interpretation*, Sheed & Ward, N. Y., 1934.

Carr, Edward H.: *Dostoyevsky*, Houghton Mifflin, Boston, 1913.

Gide, André: *Dostoyevsky*, Knopf, New York, 1926.

Gide, André: *Dostoyevsky*, New Directions, 1949.

Kaus, Otto: *Dostojewsky und sein Schicksal*, Laub, Berlin, 1923.

Lloyd, J. A.: Dostoevsky, a great Russian realist, Paul, London, 1913.

Mackiewitz, Stanilaw: Dostoevsky, Orbis, London, 1948.

Meier-Graefe: Dostoevsky, the Man and his Work, Harcourt, 1928.

Merezhkovsky, Dmitry S.: Tolstoy und Dostoyevsky, Voegel, Berlin, 1919.

Fueloep-Miller, René: Dostojewskys Handschriften (*Der unbekannte Dostojewsky*), Piper, Muenchen, 1926.

Fueloep-Miller, René: Die Krisis in Dostojewskys Leben (*Dostojewsky am Roulette*), Piper, Muenchen, 1925.

Fueloep-Miller, René: *Dostojewskys heilige Krankheit*, Wissen und Leben, Zuerich, 1926.

Fueloep-Miller, René and Eckstein, Friedrich: Dostojewskys unbekannter Nachlass, 10 volumes, Piper, Muenchen, 1926–1929.

Fueloep-Miller, René and Eckstein, Friedrich (edited): *Lebenserinnerungen der Gattin Dostojewskys*, Piper, Muenchen, 1925.

Fueloep-Miller, René and Eckstein, Friedrich (edited): Raskolnikows Tagebuch, Piper, Muenchen, 1928.

Powys, John Cooper: *Dostoyevsky*, J. Lane, London, 1946.

Roe, Ivan: *The Breath of Corruption*, Hutchinson, London, 1946.

Roubiczek, Paul: *The Misinterpretation of Man*, Scribners, N. Y., 1947.

Simmons, Ernest J.: *Dostoyevsky, the Making of a Novelist*, Oxford Un. Pr., 1946.

Soloviov, Yevgeni, A.: *Dostoyevsky, His Life and Literary Activity*, Allen & Unwin, London, 1916.

Suarés, André: *Dostoyevsky*, Paris, 1911.

Troyat, Henri: *Firebrand*, Roy, N. Y., 1946.

Vogüe, Eugene, M.: *The Russian Novelists*, Lothrop Co., Boston, 1887.

Yarmolinsky, A. T.: *Dostoyevsky*, Harcourt, 1934.

Zweig, Stefan: *Master Builders*, Viking Press, N. Y., 1930.

Dostoyevsky, F. M.: *Collected Novels*, Modern Library, Random House, N. Y.

Dostoyevsky, F. M.: *Diary of a Writer*, Scribners, N. Y., 1949.

SELECTIVE INDEX

DOSTOEVSKY'S WORKS

DOSTOEVSKY'S CHARACTERS

POLITICAL NAMES

POLITICAL CONCEPTS

VARIOUS WORDS

VARIOUS NAMES

NINETEENTH AND TWENTIETH CENTURY AUTHORS AND THEIR WORKS